Seasoned with Peace

Spring

Practical help for becoming a biblical, prayerful, playful peacemaker

Compiled by Susan Mark Landis, Lisa J. Amstutz, Cindy Snider, and Judith Baer Kulp

Design by Cynthia Friesen Coyle

Mennonite Press Inc • Newton, KS • 2011

Library of Congress Control Number: 2011902138

ISBN 978-0-9830416-1-0

Book Design | Cynthia Friesen Coyle

Printing | Mennonite Press of Newton, KS

Deb,
Many thanks for your kindness & patience. May all your life be seasoned with peace.

Susan

Dedicated to *you*
to support your decision to be a peacemaker,
because we're all in this together.

—*from the dozens of us who donated our time to create this book*—

black bean relish   75
lemon vinaigrette   54
oatmeal muffins   195
                      246
eggplant

Table of contents

Our purposes in publishing this book are twofold:

- To make available in a different medium entries previously published in *PeaceSigns* over the past six years and the weekly prayers for peace over the past three years.
- To raise money for Mennonite peace and justice work.

To receive free copies of the prayers and *PeaceSigns*,
see **http://peace.mennolink.org/getinvolved.html**

Introduction

During our Sunday school class discussion this week, someone sounded sad that we weren't first generation Christians—that having been brought up in Christian homes and never had dramatic conversions, we didn't have the excitement to share our faith that others have.

But I need a near-daily conversion to choose to follow Jesus. When a friend and I are not communicating well, I have to take a deep breath and ask Jesus to help me show love, rather than prove myself correct. When I'm traveling and grumpy about delays, I have to will myself to care about the people around me rather than my place in line. When I obstinately want to consume more and better things "because I'm worth it," I have to remember the millions who have so much less than I do, and that I won't be able to share with them if I spend a lot on myself. And you know, it's fun to share!

Daily conversions perhaps aren't dramatic, but I find them necessary. Day after day, I am transformed closer to the image of Jesus, who taught us to love, make peace, and seek justice. And then I get busy and harassed and slide backward and need grace from God and those around me. I also need a community to help me again choose to seek Jesus.

Working with *Seasoned with Peace* has provided me much of that community. Dozens of volunteers have taken the time to think about how to follow Jesus' way of peace and have shared their thoughts, photos, recipes, crafts, and prayers to also help you. In a sense, they are sharing the excitement of their own daily conversions, their own learnings and joy as they decide to follow Jesus. They chose to do this because your journey matters to them: we're all in this together.

All who worked on this book are committed to learning more about Jesus' path to peace. Some are considering new ideas about who God is and taking the risk to share those thoughts with you. Some believe that we can learn from people of other religious traditions; that other eyes sometimes help us see ourselves better. You needn't agree with everyone in this book, but we hope their ideas will give you food for thought and perhaps open some paths that lead to growth.

Please take a moment and send a note to peaceforallseasons@gmail.com and let us know which entries you especially appreciate. We'll send your note on as thanks to the folks who have so generously given of their time. If you'd like to discuss an idea further with a writer, we'll be glad to get you in touch. And watch our blog, www.seasonedwithpeace.com, for additional entries and the news of our next publication, SUMMER!

May the Creator of the seasons bless your spring with seeds of peace,
May the gentle rain of God's Spirit cause them to burst forth, and
May the light of Christ's love nourish them with all that is loving and good.

—*Susan Mark Landis*

A bouquet of never-fading fragrant spring blooms to:

- Judith Baer Kulp, who appeared via Facebook and brought expertise, wisdom, and wit to our seasons;
- Lisa Amstutz, who cares about details and rarely sleeps; and
- Cindy Snider, who is our chief cheerleader.

Special thanks to:

Carol Penner, whose prayer-poems and photos create memorable images; and Duane Ediger, Lora Steiner, and Carol Honderich whose eyes and hands made a difference.

April

"Live in each season as it passes;

breathe the air,

drink the drink,

taste the fruit."

— Henry David Thoreau

Carol Penner

"Humor and laughter are not necessarily the same thing.
Humor permits us to see into life from a fresh and gracious perspective.
We learn to take ourselves more lightly in the presence of good humor.
Humor gives us the strength to bear what cannot be changed and the
sight to see the human under the pompous."

—Joan Chittister

Holding on to joy

*"Go and enjoy choice food and sweet drinks, and send some to those who have
nothing prepared. This day is holy to our Lord.
Do not grieve, for the joy of the Lord is your strength."*

—Nehemiah 8:10 (NIV)

I remember many songs from my childhood that contain the word joy. From
simple little ditties like "I've Got the Joy, Joy, Joy, Joy, Down in My Heart"
to "Joy is Flowing Like a River," and "The Joy of the Lord," the list is quite
long. But what does joy really mean when it comes to peace and justice work?

This question is dear to me because I have observed an inordinate number of
so-called peacemakers who are so serious about their calling that they forget to
exhibit any sense of joy at all, let alone the possibility of an outright guffaw. Oh,
I know peacemaking is serious work (and work it is), and how the associated
trials and tribulations weigh on one's soul. It seems impossible to have joy when
there is so much suffering, anger, violence, and hatred in this world.

Yet I believe it is not only possible but necessary to find our underlying joy
in these situations.

One only need look at some of the most difficult situations in the world to
find people who understand the unmitigated joy of the Lord. Take, for example,
Nelson Mandela, a man who was imprisoned for over 25 years because he was
an active anti-apartheid peacemaker. Did his joy vanish during his imprisonment? Not a chance. Is this the joy of the Lord of which we speak?

It is my belief that peacemakers need three character traits, or gifts, to
survive in their arduous work: wisdom, humility, and a sense of humor (from
deep-seated joy). Surely there is nothing funny about disparate groups trying to
kill each other; a situation often encountered by Christian Peacemaker Teams.
Nor is the desperation of water-deprived, transient, weather-beaten immigrants
something to celebrate.

Nonetheless, people who interact with this disenfranchised and forgotten
segment of humanity need not give up their joy. Nor do they have to appear

happy all the time. Sometimes things are rotten and it is not the moment for smiling—but the joy of the Lord has not abandoned us.

I am convinced that like great music, wonderful art, or natural beauty, the joy of the Lord must surely endure through the deepest of disasters. It is one of those wonderful lights that cannot be extinguished.

—Jep Hostetler

Action steps

Try a little foolishness

April 1 fell on a Saturday one year when my children were in preschool and we cared for neighborhood children. A celebration was in order. When the children gathered around the table for lunch, they found their plates upside-down. "You may not have the rest of your meal until you have finished your dessert!" I proclaimed, setting a brownie on each plate. This became an annual ritual. One year at a church potluck someone whispered to me with concern that my children were eating only dessert on upside-down plates.

Traditions help define a family. People who had suffered from war sometimes sat at our table, but we all enjoyed a bit of foolishness together.

—Susan Mark Landis

Loving our enemies with prayer

"You have heard that it was said,
'You shall love your neighbor and hate your enemy.' But I say to you,
love your enemies and pray for those who persecute you."

—Matthew 5:43-44 (NRSV)

While we may understand this command of Jesus and affirm the concept of loving enemies as the right thing to do, we may not have thought much about what this means in our own lives. On the very personal level, we should think about how we treat those who seek to do us some sort of harm—at home, at work, or in our neighborhood. Such people certainly could be considered our "enemies." This is important and necessary.

But perhaps just as necessary is to think about how to love those who have declared themselves to be our enemies, or perhaps those whom our government has designated as enemies.

As fallen people, we tend to see the world as divided into two groups: the "good guys" and the "bad guys." We, of course, are good, and those who are against us (terrorists, insurgents, nations that do not support our national policies, nations with types of governments or religions different from ours) are bad. While we may understand that we need to "turn the other cheek" or "go the extra mile" with some specific person who is wronging us, we may not understand how to love a more vague enemy, one whom we consider to be one of the "bad guys."

Realistically, most of us will probably never come face-to-face with a terrorist. Nevertheless, one important and effective thing we can do to love our enemies, that in fact Jesus instructs us to do, is to pray for them. As a church, we are quick to pray for our leaders, our country, and even for our troops. Seldom, it seems, do we pray for our enemies.

We can pray for enemies individually in our personal devotional time and in congregations during corporate prayer. Prayers for enemies should be for their well-being, now and eternally. Our prayers are one way to express love for our enemies and to make peace with them, seeking both to foster their peace with God and our mutual peace with each other.

—*Tom Beutel*

A prayer for enemies

Lord God, Creator, Sustainer, Deliverer,
We pray for those who would do us harm; those who would call
    themselves our enemies.
Help us to understand how we may be provoking their hatred.
Help us to understand the frustration or desperation that leads them to
    strike out.
Help us to love them and not to hate, to bless and not to curse.
We ask that your presence be with those who embrace and practice
    violence against others.
We do not ask that you would assist them in their aggressive actions,
    but that you would open their eyes to your love.
We ask that you would help us to forgive them, and for them to forgive us.
We ask that you would soften their hearts and lead them to peace
    with you and with all others.
Then, perhaps in our lifetime, we could call each other
    brothers and sisters in Christ.

Amen.

—*Tom Beutel*

"A peacemaker prays. Prayer is the beginning and the end, the source and the fruit, the core and the content, the basis and the goal for all peacemaking. I say this without apology, because it allows me to go straight to the heart of the matter, which is that peace is a divine gift, a gift we receive in prayer.

Prayer and resistance, the twin pillars of Christian peacemaking, are two interlocking ways of giving expression to our life in the dwelling place of God. They come from the same source and lead to the same goal."

—Henri Nouwen

Judith Baer Kulp

The endless song

And I heard a sound from heaven like the roar of rushing waters
and like a loud peal of thunder.
The sound I heard was like that of harpists playing their harps.
And they sang a new song before the throne
and before the four living creatures and the elders.

—Revelation 14:2-3a (NIV)

I board the train at the West End Station in downtown Dallas. An older, whiskered man boards and sits across the aisle. His appearance, the way he holds his hands, betrays a state of mental illness or disability. I hesitate to start a conversation, doubting my ability not to insult him through condescension.

As the train pulls out from the station, he softly intones a song that relaxes me—body, mind, and spirit. His soul, his sanity, he has shown, are not lost. Beauty still has a home in him. Over the Trinity River, his melody dances through the train car. A half mile before my stop, humming softer than he and in his key, I fill in during his inhales. His volume increases. He has heard me. We make harmony. I see his reflection in the window. He is looking at me. He says something I don't understand. I tell him his music is beautiful. He speaks again. Again I don't understand.

Finally he is intelligible. He tells me he is going to the Veterans Hospital. "I am a Vietnam veteran," he says.

"That's been a long time ago," I say.

"Thirty years. I'm still suffering from that war," he says.

"War is hard on people," I say.

He clarifies, "They give you a gun and tell you to go shoot women and children."

"Your military superiors?" I ask.

"Yes," he says emphatically, and pauses. "I can still hear their screams."

The train approaches my stop. "I will pray for you," I offer.

"You are a Christian?" he asks.

"Yes."

"So am I. I need to be forgiven," he says.

The train comes to a halt. Stepping out, I say, "You are already forgiven."

The door still open, through the window he tells me, "It doesn't come easy."

"Your enemies forgive you," I dare to offer.

"It's hard to forgive myself," he says.

"Just know that your enemies have already forgiven you."

The door shuts. The train moves on. Three stops later, his booty of pain and beauty will echo down the corridors of the Veterans Hospital: a plaintive song a third of a century long, searching, still searching for the ears his obedience shut.

—Duane Ediger

April 4

Tender sprouts

You answer us with awesome and righteous deeds,
God our Savior, the hope of all the ends of the earth and of the farthest seas,
who formed the mountains by your power,
having armed yourself with strength, who stilled the roaring of the seas,
the roaring of their waves, and the turmoil of the nations.
The whole earth is filled with awe at your wonders; where morning dawns, where
evening fades, you call forth songs of joy.

—Psalm 65: 5-8 (NIV)

O God,
for too long the world
has called us to war,
and our dead lie sprawled
across the bleeding centuries.
But you
break the bow and shatter the spear,
calling us to sow the seeds of peace
in the midst of despair.
In tenderness,
may we take the tiniest sprouts
and plant them
where they can safely grow
into blossoms of hope.
Amen.

—Linea Reimer Geiser

Tender sprouts of asparagus are among spring's earliest delicacies.
Fresh asparagus is delicious and simple to prepare.

Roasted Asparagus

Preheat oven to 400 ° F.

Wash desired amount of asparagus and snap off the ends; they'll naturally break at the right point.

Pat dry with dish towel, avoiding paper towels if at all possible (after all, you've just cleaned the asparagus, right?).

Use baking pan large enough to hold all asparagus in a single layer.

Drizzle small amount of olive oil over asparagus, then salt and pepper. If you're feeling feisty, crushed red pepper flakes are spectacular.

Roll asparagus all around to evenly coat with oil and seasoning.

Roast until intensely green and charred in parts; 10-15 minutes, depending on thickness of asparagus.

Shake pan to roll spears when asparagus is about half roasted.

Enjoy as is or sprinkle with grated Parmesan cheese.

—Audrey Hindes DiPalma

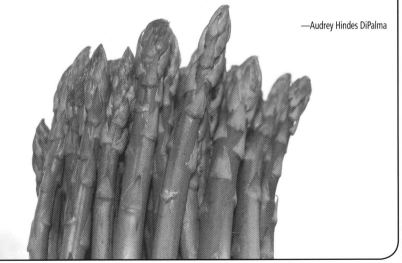

April 5

Will you harbor me?

But Jesus bent down and started to write on the ground with his finger.

—John 8:6b (NIV)

My parents once took our family on a vacation in southern Ohio, where we visited homes that had welcomed people escaping slavery on the Underground Railroad. As elementary school children, my brother and I became obsessed with the idea that surely our very old farmhouse had also been used for such purposes. We knocked on all the walls, searching for secret chambers.

The idea of offering refuge caught my imagination again as a young teen when I read *The Hiding Place*, the story of a Dutch Christian family accepting great risk to provide protection for Jewish people. I wished that my own family would have had an opportunity to do something like that.

And then, with our own children, we found ourselves in need of refuge.

We were living in Indonesia in October of 2001 as the United States moved closer to the invasion of Afghanistan. Militant Muslims expressed their outrage about the situation by threatening to sweep all Americans out of Central Java. During that time, Pak Mibsam and Ibu Rina, our Muslim neighbors, assured us that they would hide our family in the safety of their home if things got dangerous for Americans.

Those families who offered a safe refuge in the time of the Underground Railroad and in *The Hiding Place* and in Indonesia didn't offer to harbor only those who believed as they believed. They harbored people simply because they were human beings created in God's image.

We have many opportunities to be a harbor for others. We can do this by offering friendship to those who are different from us or to those who are on the fringes.

We don't have to agree on every belief or behavior. If we can welcome and love all people, and especially those who may not be welcomed or accepted by others, then we become a safe harbor in the way that Jesus became a refuge for the woman accused of adultery.

—*Jeanne Zimmerly Jantzi*

Courtesy of Capetown Travel

Praise the Lord. Praise the Lord from the heavens;
praise him in the heights above.

—Psalm 148:1 (NIV)

Praying on a windy day

On this wind-swept day
my prayer is a kite
rising from outstretched arms
stringing taut and fast
up with sailing clouds
up with soaring hawks
my kite swoops
in the high blue
writing thank you
thank you.

—Carol Penner

April 6

No secrets here

"…Be quiet for now, my sister; he is your brother. Don't take this thing to heart."
And Tamar lived in her brother Absalom's house, a desolate woman.

—2 Samuel 13:20b (NIV)

Secrets. They're complicated things. Especially for kids. Kids are told to keep secrets about Christmas gifts for siblings and surprise birthday parties for parents. They're told to keep secrets about the hiding place for a house key and the password for their facebook account.

And yet, when a friend invites them to try drugs "just this once" or an uncle touches them inappropriately, we expect them to know that these are secrets they shouldn't keep. This is especially difficult because the friend or uncle may be quite persuasive, saying things like, "No one needs to know," or "Your mom will be mad," or "I'll give you that pretty necklace we saw at the store."

What are kids to do?

How are they to know which secrets to keep and which ones to tell?

We need to establish cultures of openness in our families and churches. Secrets should never hurt anyone. If children or youth feel uncomfortable about something, they need to have a parent or other trusted adult that they can talk to about it. And we need to listen to them. Listening takes time, and sometimes it takes courage. We need to stand ready to protect our kids.

Although the media may lead us to believe otherwise, most kids who are hurt are hurt by someone they know—a parent, a neighbor, a coach, a cousin. We need to be the eyes and ears for our children. We need to be protective of our children without instilling them with fear and distrust. And we need to seek help immediately if we realize that it's we who are crossing the boundary and hurting a child. When it comes to our kids, we cannot afford to keep secrets that are doing them harm.

If you haven't read 2 Samuel for a while, go back and read the tragic story of Tamar. Starting in chapter 13, you'll read of the havoc caused when she was sexually abused. She was violated by someone she knew, and well-meaning family members told her to keep it a secret. In the end, this secrecy only confounded her pain and brought further damage to her family.

Especially during April, a month set aside for child abuse prevention, let's do all we can to protect children and strengthen families. Let's put boundaries in place that keep children safe and yet still welcome those who are not yet known to us. Jesus speaks to us of welcoming the stranger while also calling on us to protect the vulnerable. Let's not leave it up to the children or youth to figure out what to keep secret and what to tell. Let's establish a culture of openness in our families and churches that allows for dialogue without fear, and invites our kids to grow and thrive.

—Jeanette Harder

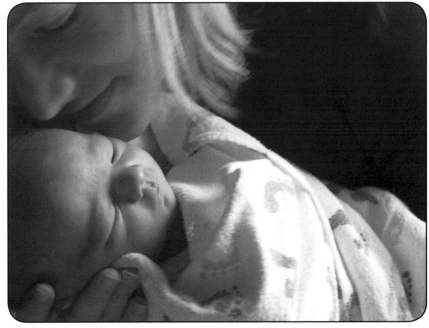

Judith Baer Kulp

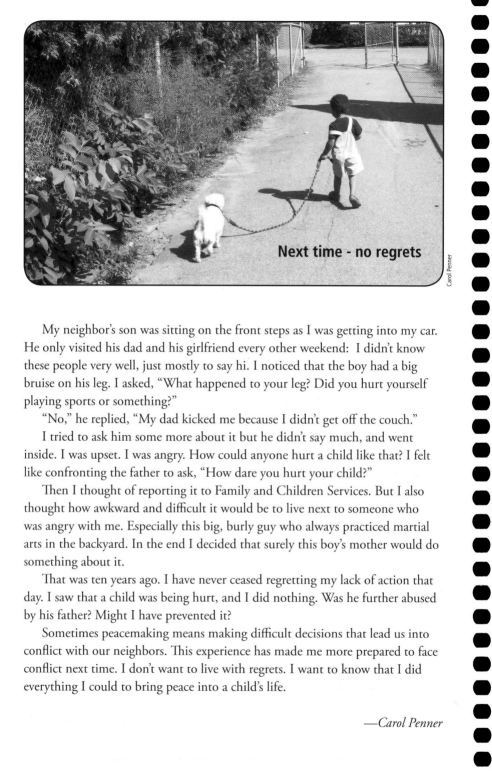

Next time - no regrets

Carol Penner

My neighbor's son was sitting on the front steps as I was getting into my car. He only visited his dad and his girlfriend every other weekend: I didn't know these people very well, just mostly to say hi. I noticed that the boy had a big bruise on his leg. I asked, "What happened to your leg? Did you hurt yourself playing sports or something?"

"No," he replied, "My dad kicked me because I didn't get off the couch."

I tried to ask him some more about it but he didn't say much, and went inside. I was upset. I was angry. How could anyone hurt a child like that? I felt like confronting the father to ask, "How dare you hurt your child?"

Then I thought of reporting it to Family and Children Services. But I also thought how awkward and difficult it would be to live next to someone who was angry with me. Especially this big, burly guy who always practiced martial arts in the backyard. In the end I decided that surely this boy's mother would do something about it.

That was ten years ago. I have never ceased regretting my lack of action that day. I saw that a child was being hurt, and I did nothing. Was he further abused by his father? Might I have prevented it?

Sometimes peacemaking means making difficult decisions that lead us into conflict with our neighbors. This experience has made me more prepared to face conflict next time. I don't want to live with regrets. I want to know that I did everything I could to bring peace into a child's life.

—*Carol Penner*

Personal lament

*It would be better to be thrown into the sea
with a millstone hung around your neck
than to cause one of these little ones to fall into sin.*

—Luke 17:2 (NLT)

My heart cries out to you, O God.
Listen to your children call to you,
Bend your ear to our pleas for help.

O God, children are dying.
Adults are hurting girls, boys, babies—doing unspeakable deeds
without regard to your judgment.
You said that it is better to hang a millstone around one's neck
than to harm a child.
Then hang millstones around the necks
of these cruel adults—bring your wrath upon them!

My heart cries out to you, O God.
Listen to the weeping of your children, O God.
Do not turn away from our pleas!

O God, I trust you to listen to your children.
I know you weep when your children weep.
I praise you for bending your heart to hear and respond to our cries, O God.

—June Mears Driedger

Theology of junk

Truly I tell you, whatever you did for one of the least of these brothers and sisters of mine, you did for me.

—Matthew 25:40 (NIV)

I have a soft spot for junk, what other people call "junk." I'm not talking about yard sale or thrift shop finds, or even being a packrat. I mean good stuff we throw away. I'm especially drawn to dumpsters and curbside piles. I actually feel sad when I see some perfectly good object that has been discarded. The other day I witnessed a couch being fed to a trash compactor and it broke my heart. It seemed so violent and unnecessary.

About two years ago, I found fabric in a dumpster in Princeton, N.J. I filled up the trunk, went home, and then went back for another load. All the old swatches of upholstery and drapery fabric from an interior decorating store had been tossed. I've made quite a few things with that fabric—an Orange Peel Quilt and other wall hangings, shoulder bags, and I have plans for the rest of it.

Before that, we found some dishes piled next to the dumpster near our apartment. They're a beautiful blue onion Nordic pattern, one we regularly see in antique stores. Someone ate their morning cereal and put it out with the rest of the dishes.

Then there was a desk. Not many desks seem to be made of real wood anymore. This one was small and charming; it had knives, forks, and spoons for drawer handles. But it was left out by the dumpster in the rain and got damaged. We tried to save it, brought it home and let it dry, but it was too far gone.

This summer I discovered a gold mine for junk. We live next to a plant nursery in Atlanta. One day I was walking past the nursery and noticed an open dumpster out back. On my way home, I stopped to peek inside, and lo! I found perfectly good plants that just needed a little extra care. I retrieved a four-foot tall hibiscus plant—I can't wait until it blooms.

I think a lot about habits. I worry about the long-term effects of them. I wonder how our psyches and worldviews are shaped by our actions, intentional and unintentional, every day. In this case, I worry about how our attitudes toward things might have a trickle-down effect on our attitude toward people and relationships. Does something happen to us when we stop fixing things, just throw them away, and get new ones? I'm afraid we already do that to each other.

What kinds of things have you thrown away in the last year? Could anything have been fixed, or given away? What about relationships? Are there any that you can still retrieve from the "junk pile"? The least of these that Jesus speaks of in Matthew 25 are all of those people that we consider burdensome, that we consider disposable, and that we'd be "better off without." But he says when we do something for the least of these, we do it for him.

Pulling things out of the dumpster and fixing things that are broken can inspire in us new vision for right relationships with one another. If there is anyone or anything teetering on the edge, it's never too late to reclaim, redeem, and restore.

—Audrey Hindes DiPalma

Otterville

Merrill R. Miller

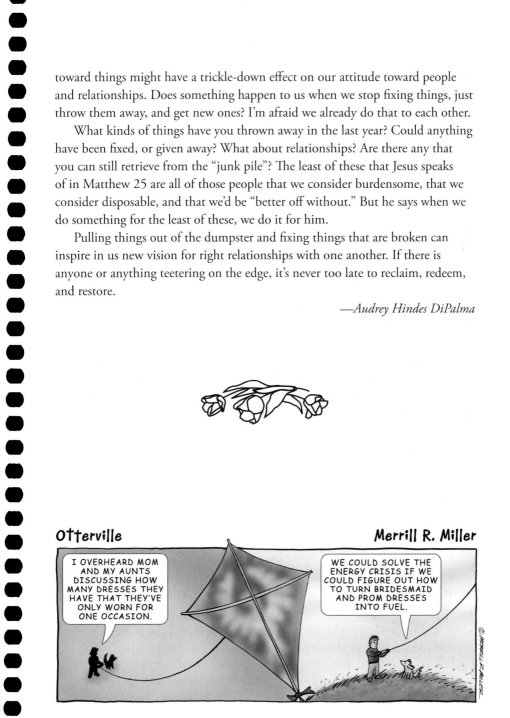

17

Orange peel wall hanging or quilt — Project guidelines

There's no true quilting in this project, so when all the pieces are as-sembled, it's done. When I used swatches of upholstery fabric that I found in the dumpster, I only had enough to use each swatch one time, resulting in a very eclectic and very fun project. Because it was upholstery fabric, I sewed 1/2" seams; if you're using something more normal like cotton, use a 1/4" seam. I also chose to keep all the dark colors on one side and all the light colors on the other side, because I like the contrast of the "peels." Arrange the pieces in any way that suits you.

Start by finding something perfectly round and sturdy to use as a tem-plate. It can be any size; the smaller the template, the more circles you'll need to cut out to achieve desired final dimensions. My template was 9" in diameter, resulting in 5 1/2" squares when the "peels" were turned down. My finished wall hanging was 6 squares by 5 squares, approxi-mately 33" x 27.5".

Once you have your template, assess your fabric situation. To help deter-mine final dimensions, use your template to trace a circle on a piece of paper. Cut it out and fold over the edges along the circumference of the circle to account for your seams. Then fold four edges of the circle over to form a perfect square. Use the width of this square to determine how many circles across and down you need. At 6 by 5 squares, I needed 60 circles; 30 light for the back to be folded over the 30 dark for the front.

Now you're ready to assign front/back pairs. Because all my fabric was different, I wanted to ensure the most contrast between pairs. With right sides together, sew around the circle with appropriate seam allowance, leaving a 1" gap. Clip around the circle so that it won't pucker when turned right side out. Use a skewer or a chopstick to push circle fully out. Press the circle with the open seam tucked in, then use a blind stitch to close it.

After all your circles have been sewn, turned right side out, and pressed, arrange them in desired order. Center paper square template on each circle and trace a line on each side with fabric marker or pencil onto circle. These lines are where the "peels" will be folded over (so the marks will never show).

Working on one row at a time, take the first two circles in that row and put them backsides together. Sew only down the line of one side. Now take your third circle and lay it with the backside against the backside of the second circle. Be sure to sew down the side that is directly opposite the two peels that were just sewn together on circles one and two—you're making a strip. Continue sewing the circles together to complete the entire row. Do each row separately so that you now have several strips.

When all your strips are completed, use the same concept of piecing the circles together to piece the rows together. It may help to pin the tips of the circles together, and sew continuously down the entire strip. Take your time at each intersection. At some places, you will sew through eight layers of fabric. I never broke a needle—even with upholstery fabric—but I went slowly.

The end is nigh! You can either sew down the peels that are flapping around by topstitching with your machine, or you can do a blind stitch by hand. I chose to do the latter. You can either fold the edges over and sew them down as well, or leave them open for a scalloped edge. If you go with the latter option, be sure not to mark the entire circle when tracing the square on top.

Stand back, admire, and pray for the least of these.

—Audrey Hindes DiPalma

April 9

Hearing wise words in strange places

The centurion replied, "Lord, I do not deserve to have you come under my roof.
But just say the word, and my servant will be healed."
—Matthew 8:8 (NIV)

"I'm not saying that every Muslim is a terrorist, but I am saying that every terrorist is a Muslim!" These words of a young leader of the fundamentalist Hindutva movement brought cheers from the angry mob gathered in an open field in the state of Gujarat, India. It was February 2002. Local Hindutva leaders were feeling powerful and invincible. Their call to drive all non-Hindus out of the state was bringing in large crowds, and local political leaders often acted in support of them.

Ahmadabad, capital of Gujarat, was home to large mixed communities of Hindus and Muslims who had been living together in relative peace for generations. They shared the same streets, shopped in the same markets, and mingled happily during festivals. They were neighbors who knew each other by name, exchanged local gossip, and felt comfortable in their ecumenical communities. That all came to an abrupt end during the early months of 2002 as rallies organized by the Hindutva fundamentalists grew in size and hostility.

As the poorer members of the Hindu communities were agitated into a frenzy, they were also given money to do the dirty work of the leaders. A short time later, the violence began. Mobs tore through the narrow streets looking for Muslim homes and businesses. Fires burned. People ran in panic, and blood flowed.

Within a few days, more than 2,000 people, almost all Muslims, including many pregnant women and small children, had been killed. Survivors gathered in makeshift camps in safe areas and waited. Many of them are still waiting—waiting for a sense of security and waiting for the government to investigate the rampage, provide compensation, and make certain such violence does not happen again.

I traveled to Gujarat with a small group of young Asians representing different countries and different religions. We met with survivors of the massacre to learn what lessons they could share with us about justice and peace. We were worried. How would they receive those of us who were Buddhist, Christian, and Hindu? Would vengeance be on their minds? Would they direct their anger against us?

Perhaps our fears were too influenced by what we would expect from our own societies, or perhaps we did not deeply believe that amidst so much terror and death we could find the seeds of forgiveness, compassion, and hope. We were kindly invited into the small temporary rooms of the Muslim survivors, given the most comfortable places to sit, and graciously offered tea and snacks. Their stories were shared quietly, but always with deep emotion. They had lost so much. Homes and businesses were burnt, but most of all they mourned the loss of their family members. Homes and businesses, they said, can be replaced, but a husband, wife, mother, or child can never be given back.

They talked of their losses with tears, but their voices were not angry as they shared. "They were our neighbors. We knew them. We used to eat and laugh together. Suddenly they turned on us. We don't know what happened to them."

The highlight of our brief sojourn with these people, who refuse to feel like victims, came during a chat with a young 17-year-old Muslim boy. He was only eleven when the mobs destroyed his house and killed his father. Now he lives in a tiny two-room house with the remaining members of his family, dreaming of one day becoming an airline pilot.

"What do you think of the Hindu people now?" we asked. "They killed your father. Don't you really hate them?"

His answer came without a moment's hesitation. "Don't say that Hindus killed my father. It wasn't Hindus. It was evil persons. When someone in your religion does something bad, do you say it was the religion that did it?" Then he repeated, "Don't say it was Hindus who did the violence. It was evil persons."

Thus, healing and reconciliation becomes possible through the words of wisdom of a young man who knows the reality and pain of violence.

His response is not unlike Jesus' response to the Roman captain who sought healing for his servant without a personal visit, but with only a word from Jesus from a distance. Jesus is astonished and replied, "…I've yet to come across this kind of simple trust in Israel, the very people who are supposed to know all about God and how God works…" (Matthew 8).

Would Jesus respond similarly to the young Muslim?

We need to listen to God's wisdom coming to us from strange places. Perhaps then, we could also become stronger disciples of God's forgiveness, compassion, and hope in a world full of vengeful, angry words. Perhaps then we would not be so easily swayed to support war by the agitated shouts of angry leaders.

—*Max Ediger*

Pull in your sails

One of the best pieces of
advice I've had came from a
friend who passed it on from
one of her friends.

"Just pull in your sails."

When someone is blowing
angry words my way, I can
choose to either turn my sails
to catch the full force, or pull
in my sails to let it blow by.

If I pull in my sails, I have
protected myself from the
gale force and have more
opportunity to consider a
peaceful response.

—*Jeanne Zimmerly Jantzi*

Roadblock of love

If anyone forces you to go one mile, go with them two miles.

—Matthew 5:41 (NIV)

During one of the days of our prayer pilgrimage, I was approached by a handful of concerned immigrants. We were in a county where law enforcement is authorized to act as immigration officers. The immigrant pilgrims were troubled because they alleged that one of our police escorts was a "racist cop." They said that he liked to harass Latino drivers by following closely behind them to make them nervous, then would wait for the smallest moving violation to pull them over and take them to jail where they faced possible deportation. The distressed immigrants wanted to know what we should do in response to his presence. As I thought of possible options, I recalled basic nonviolence theology, which states that without a prophetic imagination we may only consider two reactions—fight or flight.

The fight option: Let's confront the officer. Let's shame him. Let's turn the focus of our public prayer into a public confrontation of a cop.

The flight option: Let's ignore him. Let's pray he won't tail you. Let's pray he won't pull you over.

But Jesus' way is neither fight nor flight. Jesus calls his followers to find a third way, what theologians call nonviolent conflict transformation. A third way came to my mind. Here's what I proposed.

A roadblock is an external show of force that causes all of us to pause. "Do I have my license on me?" "Where's my insurance card?" "Yikes, I don't have my seatbelt on." Immigrants who cannot legally acquire a driver's license know all about roadblocks. For them, roadblocks can be terrifying experiences. "Will I go to jail?" "Will my car be towed?" "Will I be deported?" "What will become of my children?"

My proposal was simple and the immigrants loved it. It was a third way. "Let's give this police officer a roadblock of love." I encouraged the scores of immigrants to shower this cop with love. Offer him water. Offer him your lunch. Every time you see him, tell him how much you appreciate that he is accompanying you on this prayerful pilgrimage. Tell him you're praying for him and his family. Tell him God loves him. Tell him you're glad you're his brother or sister in Christ.

The countenances of the once-concerned immigrants were transformed.

The cop was stopped by a roadblock of love and was detained for the duration of the walk.

We didn't fight the cop, nor did we flee.

Will the police officer act differently when he encounters an immigrant, unable to get a license, who is driving?

We don't know. But our actions were faithful, redemption was offered, and the seeds of justice were sown.

—Anton Flores-Maisonet

Anton Flores-Maisonet

The whites of their eyes

Jesus replied: "'Love the Lord your God with all your heart and with all your soul and with all your mind.'"
This is the first and greatest commandment.

—Matthew 22:37-38 (NIV)

Earlier this week a coworker plopped into a chair in my office and asked for suggestions on an article she was writing. I gave it a quick skim and realized how hard the topic was. I wanted to be encouraging. I told her she had a good start. A few hours later on my computer screen, I looked over her completed article and began picking it apart. After sending off an email, I wondered why none of those ideas had occurred to me when we talked in person.

It didn't take me long to realize that when I looked my friend in the eyes, I didn't want to be critical. I wanted to find as much to compliment as possible. But when I was staring at a computer screen, I was more analytical and didn't mince words or ideas.

Lately I've been concerned about the way we communicate with each other in our church and in our country. Civil discourse–the ability to discuss ideas and abstract concepts without getting personal–has taken a backseat to nasty emails, bricks through the window, marches, and tirades. Part of this can be blamed on talk radio, part on the ease of email, part on fear of people different from us. But a great deal may be people's unwillingness to learn to know other people. It's easier to treat them as obstacles, or that good old-fashioned term, enemies.

People have different ways of responding to conflict, depending on whether the issue or the relationship is of most value to them at the time. I wonder if people are deciding that issues matter more than relationships. And I wonder what Jesus has to say about that. The answer isn't easy.

We know that Jesus did some name calling. In Matthew 23, he calls several groups hypocrites, snakes, vipers, and white-washed sepulchers. We also know that Jesus summed up the law by saying, "Love the Lord your God with every thing you have and your neighbor as yourself" (Matthew 22:37-38). The formula I've not been able to create would tell me when it is okay to name call and when I must show the love and understanding I'd like to receive.

Recently Ed Olfert, a Prince Albert, Saskatchewan, newspaper columnist, wrote that "Folks go through life doing the best they can." Olfert bases this claim on his belief that "the God we invoke in our solemn and sad times also has equal investment and compassion with every hurting spirit." I'm still struggling with whether I can believe this bit of wisdom, but I'm considering giving it a try. I suppose what I'm weighing is whether I'm willing to offer others the grace I hope they offer me, and that God gives me freely.

When I teach a workshop or preach a sermon, I try to remember that at least one person in the audience is dealing with deep pain (divorce, death), one has had a family argument in the car on the way to the meeting, one has a bit of a headache or nausea, and one has work tensions. That has given my words more of a compassionate, invitational bend. We all have problems aplenty that hinder our ability and energy to be the people we know God calls us to be.

When I can look into people's eyes—when I can see their pain and confusion, their hopes and dreams—I tend to be more encouraging and less critical. The next step for me is to be aware of this also when I send email or letters. People often respond better and try harder when they know that I am on their side and that I hope the best for them. That's certainly how I want to be treated; perhaps that's how my "neighbors" also want to be treated.

Don't worry; I'm not suggesting that we stop prophetically telling the truth. But I am wondering how to say it so that we invite people to consider what we are saying, rather than turn them away.

Next time, I'll try not to criticize until I see the whites of their eyes.

—*Susan Mark Landis*

Chocolate-lover's delight

We don't see the eyes of the people who harvest our chocolate. If we did, we would notice that many of the eyes belong to children who should be in school. Consider using fairly traded chocolate products.

Ingredients

1/3 cup Equal Exchange Fair Trade baking cocoa
4 tablespoons cooking oil
3/4 cup granulated sugar
1/4 teaspoon salt
1 teaspoon vanilla
1 cup flour
2 teaspoons baking powder
1/2 cup milk
1/2 cup chopped walnuts

Topping

1/2 cup granulated sugar
1/2 cup brown sugar
4 tablespoons Equal Exchange Fair Trade baking cocoa
1 cup water

Combine oil, cocoa, sugar, salt, and vanilla. Add flour and baking powder alternately with milk. Stir in walnuts. Pour into an 8 X 8 X 2" square greased pan.

Mix topping sugars and cocoa. Sprinkle over the batter in the pan. Pour 1 cup water over the top of all.

Bake at 350 ° F. for 50 minutes or until center tests set. (This comes out looking like brownies with chocolate sauce.) Serve warm with plain cream or vanilla ice cream. Serves 8.

—from http://equalexchange.coop, used by permission

Morning has broken

In the beginning when God created the heavens and the earth,
the earth was a formless void and darkness covered the face of the deep,
while a wind from God swept over the face of the waters.
Then God said, "Let there be light;" and there was light.
And God saw that the light was good;
and God separated the light from the darkness.
God called the light Day, and the darkness he called Night.
And there was evening and there was morning, the first day.

—Gen 1:1-5 (NRSV)

For those of us in the Northern Hemisphere, spring is all around us now, bursting out of every nook and cranny in the earth and making every tree, bush, shrub, flower, and blade of grass sing a new song of its own creation—a song that is filled with the hope of God, the promise of resurrection, and the work of peace.

At this time of year, I always think of the hymn "Morning Has Broken," whose words were written by Eleanor Farjeon in 1931 and made popular by Cat Stevens in 1972. To me this hymn actually sounds like spring, like hope, like God's creation.

It is the third verse that always, in particular, moves me:

> Mine is the sunlight!
> Mine is the morning
> born of the one light
> Eden saw play!
> Praise with elation,
> praise every morning,
> God's re-creation
> of the new day!

This hymn, a prayer really, means so much to me.

The idea that I am a part of God's creation, and that God shares all of that creation with me, as in the sunlight, as in the morning, is exhilarating and is never experienced quite so well as during the springtime.

But it is the idea of God's recreating the new day each and every day that gives me the ultimate hope for peace and pushes me on to work for peace, even when it seems that all hope should be lost.

The creation is a work in progress, and we human beings, as part of that work in progress, are being remade each and every day.

The more we pray for, live into, and work for peace, the more peace becomes re-created in the new day.

So perhaps today, this new day, join me in praying the words of this hymn as your own, remembering that God's will for us is to be continually reborn into that one light, the light of peace.

—*Brother James Dowd*

Otterville   Merrill R. Miller

April 13

All the time?

You show your gratitude through your generous offerings
to your needy brothers and sisters,
and really toward everyone.

—2 Corinthians 9:12 (NIV)

On the Megabus from Chicago to Minneapolis, God's word to me could not have been more explicit. There, scrawled in huge letters on the side of a barn in rural Wisconsin: "Care for others all the time."

Almost immediately, God gave me a test to see whether I was listening. The woman sitting next to me on the bus needed my help.

"Can I use your cell phone?" she asked. Hers had run out of minutes and she needed to call her bank to see whether her debit card had any available funds to recharge her phone. It didn't. In fact, she had a deficit in her account.

So, during the trip, Avery used my cell phone for numerous calls to family and friends. I heard her talking with a friend about whether they had enough cash between them to put gas in the car so they could visit a sick friend. In another call, she asked a daughter whether she had anything to eat today.

"Love others as you love yourself," we hear over and over in the New Testament. Avery apparently had little, but she was loving others with what little she had.

Paul puts it this way in 2 Corinthians 9: "You show your gratitude (to God) through your generous offerings to your needy brothers and sisters." We are all in need, of course, one way or another, but here, Paul is talking about helping those with physical needs.

Father Andrew Greeley, in his novel *The Senator and the Priest*, says that the poor are the people who cut our lawns, collect our garbage, clean our homes, and empty our bedpans. They have no life insurance, no health insurance, no pension plans, and they can't get medical care. They are the people all around us, but we don't see them.

So there I was, just a few days later, waiting outside at midnight for the return bus from Minneapolis to Chicago. It was bitterly cold and the bus was over an hour late.

A taxi driver offered a warm seat to a mother and her young child while they waited. A couple shared their thermos of hot coffee with an older man who had only a thin jacket to keep the cold out. Had these people read 1 John already and realized that the test of loving God is loving people? Or maybe they had seen the same barn sign, "Care for others all the time." Either way, I think God will probably continue testing my listening skills.

—Ron Byler

Action steps

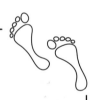

Plan to care

1. Plan specific time in your day to care for others. One day might only have enough extra time to write someone a note. Another day there might be time for a visit. PUT IT ON YOUR CALENDAR. We are people of the calendar, and what is not on the calendar is not done.

2. When you are in public places, cultivate an attitude of openness to the people around you. If you are commuting on public transportation, a casual, "Hi. I'm Susan. Are you going home? or to work?" lets the person sitting next to you know that you are a willing conversation partner. If neither of you are in the mood to talk, be aware of the noises around you. Pray for the parent coping with a tired child, for the persons muttering to themselves, for the teens bopping to their music. Each is a child of God faced with difficult life situations.

—Susan Mark Landis

Living the alternative wisdom of Jesus

Looking at his disciples, he said:
"Blessed are you who are poor, for yours is the kingdom of God.
Blessed are you who hunger now, for you will be satisfied.
Blessed are you who weep now, for you will laugh.
Blessed are you when people hate you, when they exclude you and insult you and
reject your name as evil, because of the Son of Man."

—Luke 6: 20-22 (NIV)

In the summer of 1982, a few months before peace activist and writer John Dear became a Jesuit priest, he visited the Holy Land to walk in the footsteps of Jesus.

"On the day I left the United States, Israel invaded Lebanon," Dear says. "When I stepped off the plane in Jerusalem, soldiers carrying machine guns searched me. I had unwittingly walked into a full-scale war."

Dear traveled around Israel for a month that summer. During his final week there, he camped out in the north along the beautiful Sea of Galilee. Dear describes his time: "Away from the crowds, I spent my days outdoors: swimming in the cool water, watching the sun rise and set, and quietly meditating on the Sermon on the Mount."

Each day Dear visited the Chapel of the Beatitudes, a small eight-sided stone church that stands on a hill overlooking the sea. He recalls sitting there one afternoon, carefully reading the familiar words inscribed on the chapel walls: Blessed are the poor. Blessed are those who mourn. Blessed are the meek. Blessed are those who hunger and thirst for justice. Blessed are the merciful. Blessed are the pure in heart. Blessed are the peacemakers. Blessed are those persecuted for the sake of justice, for Jesus. Love your enemies. Be as compassionate as God.

Dear says, "I walked onto the balcony and surveyed the magnificent Sea of Galilee. It suddenly dawned on me: I think Jesus is serious."

Throughout the gospels, Jesus used the traditional forms of wisdom literature to subvert and undermine the world of conventional wisdom. The purpose of his teachings was to draw his listeners into deeper reflection on life and its meaning. At the heart of Jesus' alternative wisdom is the merciful and generous God. The abundant life in God's kingdom includes loving one's enemies, being compassionate and forgiving, and rejecting the way of violence and revenge.

According to Mennonite theologian Lydia Harder, "This meant following the path that Jesus also took to the halls of power, claiming an alternative wisdom based on God the creator, sustainer, and loving parent of the universe and on the kingdom that this God was bringing to earth. Thus, in Jesus' teachings, the law, the prophetic, and the wise come together through the merciful and generous actions of Jesus and his willingness to suffer and return good for evil."

Paying attention to the wisdom of Jesus means noting how he used his power in healing; his reasoning within his teachings, in confrontation with the institutional leaders; and his compassion in overcoming the boundaries that segregated people from each other. Jesus' alternative wisdom challenged the conventional wisdom of his day, and he challenges the conventional wisdom of our day.

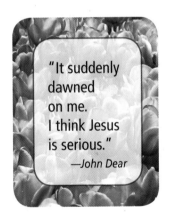

"It suddenly dawned on me. I think Jesus is serious."
—*John Dear*

As followers of Jesus, we must think and act according to this alternative wisdom, of living life as God intended life to be lived. It is a logic that is different and distinct from the power calculations of our social, economic, and political institutions.

As followers of Jesus, we look for signs of God's activity in the world and we align ourselves with the direction that we see God moving within our society and our world at large.

Writer Alyce McKenzie describes how she was driving on an interstate "so devoid of scenery that I was actually excited to see a billboard. It had a picture of Jesus with long auburn hair and blue eyes and the question, "Where will you spend eternity?" writ large. Someone had spray-painted over that question "How will you live today?"

I want to live Jesus' way.

We respond to "God of peace"

—*June Mears Driedger*

Blessed are those who hunger and thirst for righteousness
Cross-stitch magnet

Instructions

The design is worked on 14-count Aida cloth with two strands of floss. Back-stitching uses single strand.

Note that the solid upright legs of the B and R in Blessed and Righteousness are outlined.

After stitching, carefully trim the edges and affix the design to a solid magnetic backing for use as a refrigerator magnet.

—Tom Beutel

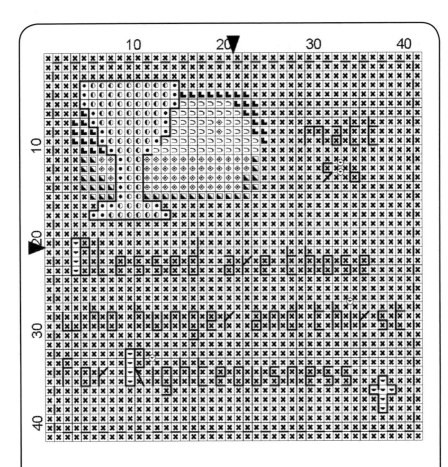

Legend:

Stitches

!	DMC 413	pewter gray - dk	Grid Size:42W x 42H
"	DMC 169	pewter - lt	Design Area:3.00″ x 3.00″
#	DMC 3371	black brown	(42 x 42 stitches)
%	DMC 433	brown - md	
$	DMC 435	brown - vy lt	
&	DMC 3045	yellow beige - dk	
'	DMC 3047	yellow beige - lt	
)	DMC 746	off white	

French Knots

DMC 3371   black brown

Back-Stitch Lines

DMC 413	pewter gray - dk
DMC 3371	black brown

What belongs to God

Give to Caesar what is Caesar's and to God what is God's.

—Matthew 22:21 (NIV)

The headline was grim, but it was the photo that made me turn away. I was in Laos in November of 2010, attending an international gathering to discuss the implementation of the treaty banning cluster munitions. The front page of the morning newspaper on November 11 featured a photo of the lifeless body of 10-year-old Poui. She had been returning home from school the day before when she innocently picked up an unexploded cluster bomblet, one of millions still left from the U.S. air war. Her older sister warned her of the danger, but when Poui discarded the bomblet, it exploded and killed her.

For more than 30 years since my wife Linda and I first went to Laos, we have heard countless stories from Lao villagers about loved ones lost or maimed by the weapons our country left behind at the end of the air war in 1973. We've seen the

Cluster bomblets are reassembled in a cluster bomb container on display at the Convention on Cluster Munitions, Lao PDR, November, 2010. Bomblets are shown scattered in grass on next page.

Titus M. Peachey

An enemy is one whose story we have not heard.

—Elinor Gene Knudsen Hoffman

bomb containers in the Lao villages which sometimes still bear the names of the U.S. companies which produced them. And we've pondered what to do.

It was a joy to help initiate a bomb removal project in Laos in 1994, an effort that now employs 1,000 workers, many of them devoted to finding and destroying the millions of bombs still left in the soil. But after 15 years of hard work, experts estimate that fewer than 1 percent of the bombs have been destroyed. And meanwhile, the United States has dropped millions more cluster munitions on Iraq and Kuwait, and hundreds of thousands on Kosovo and Afghanistan.

As I think about the small crowd gathered around Jesus one day to trap him on the question of taxes for the emperor, I envision those suffering from the world's wars as part of the circle. They are all there: children with stumps for legs, farmers without hands, warriors suffering the mental and emotional trauma of combat, people with bodies ravaged by exposure to Agent Orange or depleted uranium, and soldiers and civilians alike mourning the incomparable loss of a child, a parent or a spouse to the terror of war.

When I view this scene in the recesses of my mind, I know that everyone in the circle belongs to God. God's image is indelibly stamped on all of their lives and ours. And just as I cannot pull the trigger or drop the bomb to destroy the image of God in others, neither can I willingly pay the emperor or my own government to do it.

And so as has been our practice these past 30 years, on April 15 we will withhold a portion of our income taxes and donate the funds instead to an agency that promotes life, justice, well-being, and peace. We will write a letter with our 1040 return, respectfully explaining our beliefs. In this very small way, we try to make sure that we give to God what belongs to God, with a clear call to the "emperor" not to destroy it.

—*Titus M. Peachey*

April 16

The world you love

God saw all that he had made, and it was very good.
And there was evening, and there was morning—the sixth day.

—Genesis 1:31 (NIV)

O God,
We are bodies, blessed and broken.
We pray for the healing touch of your Spirit upon us.
We pray you touch our loved ones who suffer illness,
Who face loneliness, dementia, death.
We pray for your healing touch upon the body of the earth.
Help us hear the groaning of your beautiful creation.
Help us walk softly upon the ground,
Breathe slowly the air we need,
Drink mindfully the water we require.
Give us wisdom, O Lord, to care for your holy work.
Help us simplify our desires, curtail our consumption,
Hold lovingly the land, water, and air you have provided.
Teach us to be your healing agents each day
As we care for the world you love.
With thanks for your abundant grace
We offer you our lives, following the way of Jesus,
Our Lord and teacher,
Alive in the power of your Holy Spirit.

Amen.

—*Gordon Houser*

April 17

The sounds of peace

Be perfect, be of good comfort, be of one mind, live in peace;
and the God of love and peace shall be with you.

—2 Corinthians 13:11 (KJV)

In 1971 and 1972, Quang Ngai was my home. Visiting this small provincial town in Central Vietnam 38 years later, I had difficulty recognizing it. Almost all of the streets are now paved and the boundaries of the town have expanded considerably. The numerous refugee camps and strategic hamlets are gone and new buildings including several large hotels have sprung up throughout the town. The small dirt path that once ran along the Tra Khuc River marking the northern boundary of the town is now a wide, tree-lined boulevard with cafes, parks, and jogging paths.

Parts of the town were still recognizable, but there was something about Quang Ngai that seemed strange and even eerie. I sat quietly looking out the window of my hotel room trying to identify the cause of this feeling of strangeness. Slowly it dawned on me. The strangeness was the silence. No, the town was not really silent. The trees near the small hotel were filled with a variety of birds singing their mating songs. Motorcycles roared by from time to time, people in the teashop across the road chatted and laughed and car horns occasionally punctuated the air with their blasts. The silence I was hearing was the absence of any sounds of war.

When I lived in Quang Ngai, the sounds of war were constant companions. Outgoing artillery fired from the American base a few blocks from our house jarred us out of our sleep and interrupted our meals. Incoming rockets caused chaos in the streets as people raced from place to place to see if their children were safe. The concussions of B-52 raids ripping the distant mountains apart shook the curtains in our house and knocked puffs of dust from the ceiling tiles. The gunfire, both distant and near, was almost as common to the people in Quang Ngai as was the chirping of birds in the trees. Warplanes of all types flew constantly over the town, rattling windows and sending the neighborhood dogs into a frenzy.

All these sounds, and many more, were now gone from life here. What I was sensing as strange was the sound of peace. What a beautiful sound for the people of Vietnam. Here in Quang Ngai, it was clear that people were thriving on this peace. There was a calm bustle about the city, people wore relaxed smiles, markets were busy and—above all—the explosive sounds of war no longer disturbed the physical and emotional lives of the children. Quang Ngai was a very poor province during the war, but now the economy is growing and, for at least most of the people, survival is no longer their main concern.

The sounds of peace are intoxicating. One has to wonder why the world has such a penchant for war. Better to listen to the wise words of Paul when he said, "…Be perfect, be of good comfort, be of one mind, live in peace; and the God of love and peace shall be with you" (2 Corinthians 13:11).

—*Max Ediger*

Max Ediger

Vietnamese Mut Dua or Candied Coconut

Tet is the most important celebration of the Vietnamese lunar calendar. It welcomes in the spring, and for at least three days families and friends celebrate with special foods, parties, and neighborhood visits. When I lived in South Vietnam, friends always brought us quantities of candied fruits as Tet gifts. These were a special treat. While many different kinds of fruits and vegetables were used, my favorite was coconut.

Ingredients

coconut
sugar
vanilla extract

Buy larger pieces of coconut rather than the shredded kind. Using a vegetable peeler, cut thin long slices of the coconut. Weigh the slices of coconut and then use sugar equal to or 3/4 the weight of the coconut.

Place the sugar and 1 1/2 tablespoons of water in a large heavy-bottomed pot or copper kettle. Set the pot over moderate heat to melt the sugar, about 3 minutes. Stir in about 1 tablespoon of vanilla and then add the coconut.

Cook, stirring constantly with a wooden spoon, over moderately low heat until all of the water evaporates and the sugar crystallizes and becomes dry, about 30 minutes. Remove and allow to cool.

—Max Ediger

April 18

A cautionary tale

From the least to the greatest, all are greedy for gain;
prophets and priests alike all practice deceit.
They dress the wound of my people as though it were not serious.
"Peace, peace," they say,
when there is no peace.

—Jeremiah 6:13,14 (NIV)

Once upon a time, a public school kindergarten teacher decided to use the language of peace in a roomful of five- and six-year-olds. These children were well versed in many of the ways of their less than nurturing world, but not in the ways of peace. Two little girls in the class, whose families were part of a peace church, caught on. They, in fact, asked the teacher if they could be a Peace Patrol during centers time, and rove around the room as a presence to promote peace in the many interactions going on during that small group activity time.

The teacher, being grateful for their insight, quickly agreed to their Peace Patrol. So one day, the Peace Patrol called the teacher's attention to a conflict between several of their classmates over who got which plastic dinosaurs to play with. As the teacher knelt down to probe the parameters of the problem with the boys involved, one of the five-year-olds stated the problem as he saw it. He then added, "And I don't want to make peace, either!"

Honesty is supposed to be the best policy, and in this case, it came right to the point. No hypocrisy here. No waste of time pretending, posturing, supposing if, or acting like peace was possible or desirable. Just a plain, "I don't want to make peace."

This event caused the kindergarten teacher to wonder. In ancient times, the prophet Jeremiah lamented over Jerusalem, "From the least to the greatest, all are greedy for gain; prophets and priests alike all practice deceit. They dress the wound of my people as though it were not serious. 'Peace, peace,' they say, when there is no peace" (Jeremiah 6:13-14).

Hmmmm. Do we often echo such actions? Do WE really want peace enough to do what it takes to achieve it? Can we lay down our greed and deceit? she pondered.

I simply cannot understand why the Palestinians and Israelis cannot reach peace. There is no reason in the world why Catholics and Protestants in Northern Ireland need to kill each other. What is wrong with those people? How can Bosnians, Serbs, Croats, and others who are always at each other's throats in Eastern Europe continue to harbor ancient grudges?" the teacher had often thought, sometimes expressed.

But now, she questioned. *Am I actually being dishonest? Do I (and others like me) really want peace, but not enough to ever give up what, in our hearts, we consider our own best interests? Until I personally am ready to give up what it takes to have peace, am I really responding like the five-year-old who retorted, 'And I don't want to make peace, either'?*

You may have guessed by now that the kindergarten teacher was me. As I have continued my journey towards truly becoming a more honest peacemaker these past 20-something years, one member of the Peace Patrol has continued her work in the context of Haiti, among other things. The other has a child of her own who will no doubt learn the ways of peace at her knee.

May God hasten the time that we say, "Peace, peace," and there will be peace. May we each attempt to be on Peace Patrol wherever we find ourselves placed in our world.

—*Beth Berry*

Action step

Be on peace patrol

Think about how you will learn to see with the eyes of a Peace Patrol rather than "minding your own business" as we are taught to do.

My brother's keeper

"Am I my brother's keeper?"

—Genesis 4:9 (NIV modified)

There is a certain deception in the sounds of peace that now flood Quang Ngai and the surrounding orchards and rice paddies. While wars do, in time, come to an end and people move forward to rebuild their lives, the legacies of those wars remain and cannot, nor should not, be forgotten. In Quang Ngai the reminders of the war linger throughout the province, but usually in places hidden from the eyes of the passing tourist.

One of the most horrific legacies left behind is something called Agent Orange. First used in Vietnam around 1961, it remains in the soil, water, fish, and, most sadly, in the bodies of many of the people.

Agent Orange was used in Vietnam to destroy crops and defoliate the jungle. From 1961 to 1970, over 21 million gallons of Agent Orange containing about 400 kilograms of dioxin were sprayed over vast areas of South Vietnam. Dioxin is one of the most toxic chemicals known to science.

When the poison was sprayed over the forests and fields, farmers in the area were directly affected. They report that when the mist settled on them, their skin became very hot. They had to wash immediately and afterward they suffered from serious skin problems. In Quang Ngai Province, some 27,000 gallons were used, destroying vast areas of plant life. I remember in 1971 driving a motorcycle through areas near the mountains where nothing green existed. All was barren. Even birds did not survive.

No warnings were given that Agent Orange might have serious negative effects on people. Even the American soldiers given the duty to store and load it into the planes prior to a spraying mission were not warned to wear protective clothing. After returning to the United States, many of them started having serious health problems. The U.S. military and government refused to admit that these problems were related to Agent Orange. Vietnam veterans and their families finally filed a class action suit against the seven chemical companies that produced Agent Orange and other chemicals used in Vietnam.

The case was settled out of court in May 1984 for victims and families of those exposed to herbicides for $180 million (the lawyers got a staggering $100 million). The amount given to qualifying families was a pittance. For example, a woman whose husband suffered and eventually died, leaving her with three children, was given just over $3,000.

However, no assistance has been given to the farmers of Vietnam. In Quang Ngai alone, some 100,000 people were exposed to the toxin and at least 16,432 have been seriously affected. Research suggests that from 3.2 to 4 million people were exposed in all of Vietnam. The farmers and soldiers who were directly in the path of the spraying suffer from a variety of health issues such as cancer, skin disease, etc. They are considered the first generation of Agent Orange victims.

Their children, the second generation, have fared much worse. A very large percent of these children are born with severe deformities. Some have enlarged heads, stunted limbs, and blindness. A number seem completely normal at birth, but as they grow older, their bones suddenly start growing in grotesque shapes until they are unable to move about on their own. In some cases, children are born and grow up in a normal way. They marry, but their sons and daughters (third generation) may have even worse deformities than the second generation. Medical evidence indicates that certain cancers, diabetes, spina bifida, and other birth defects are attributable to the exposure.

Often the first generation victims die from their health problems, leaving a destitute mother or father to try to care for the invalid sons and daughters. When asked if they thought things would improve in the fourth generation they admitted to being doubtful.

The dioxins are in the soil and the water. They accumulate in fish and in the fatty tissue of cows and pigs. With the poisons in the food chain and possibly damaging the genetic makeup of the people, the problem may last far into the future.

Again, the voice of Cain becomes our own voice, "Am I my brother's keeper?" (Genesis 4:9).

—Max Ediger

April 20

Our boys

April 20 is the remembrance
of the shooting at Columbine High School
in Colorado in 2004.

Likely you remember that day and the impact it had on your life every bit as clearly as I do. Each spring when my columbine flowers push up in the garden and the Mars-like blossoms burst forth, I pause to remember the horror of kids shooting kids.

The shooting happened midweek. On Friday I was scheduled to present a seminar on teaching peace to children for a community mental health day. I had only presented these materials in congregational settings, so I had been struggling with how to edit them for a secular audience. Now I wondered how the shooting would change us all.

My seminar room was the dining area of a children's group home. By the time I began presenting, the chairs were full, the floor was full, and people were sitting on the stairway. I looked at all the stricken faces and knew I couldn't give them what they longed to learn.

"When the boys are armed and in the woods, it's too late to teach peace," I said, gulping back tears. "We need to emphasize peace as our children are growing up, teach them ways of dealing with conflict that are acceptable. Likely we're already doing some of that. Let's list what we're already doing and then I'll add some ideas."

I turned to the whiteboard to begin the list. The room was silent. I thought I hadn't communicated well. "Think a minute. What are the ways you already are helping children realize the importance of peacemaking, dealing with their anger, and good conflict resolution?" The bewilderment deepened. Finally one person said, "I don't think that ever occurred to me." As one, the group nodded.

During the next hour the group soaked up ideas about teaching peace to children. Afterward I was mobbed. "Will you come work with our bus drivers?

They don't know how to deal with fights on the bus." "Can you give an in-service at our school?" "Will you present at our men's retreat?"

I had been shoved out of my cocoon and was blinking at the bright light of reality. Our public school employees had never considered emphasizing peace and wanted to learn.

That week of the shootings, I learned that once the boys are in the woods, it is too late. Secondly, I realized that many people in our communities care, but don't have the tools to help children learn about peacemaking.

The third thing I learned is that those boys in the woods are our boys. Each child in my community matters to my family because their unhappiness is our unhappiness. They are mine—the bully of the classroom, the children from the unstable family that occasionally show up at church, the kids hanging out downtown with nowhere to go. Our lives intersect whether we know each other's names or not. They are all our children.

—Susan Mark Landis

Carol Penner

Columbine – courtesy Betty Ford Alpine Gardens

Call to worship

Come, Lord Jesus, and converse with us,
as you did with the disciples on the road to Emmaus.
Teach us your ways, as you patiently opened the scriptures for them.
Teach us how to be your people in our congregations.
Teach us how to form relationships with the rulers of our country.
As the disciples walked together on that road,
give each of us listening friends with whom we can discuss these issues,
because we swim in a patriotic and emotional ocean
and can easily not recognize you,
our Christ of peace.

Amen.

Closing of worship

Teach us, Lord, to hail only your name,

for you alone have true power.
When we need security to walk through the uncertainties of this world,
remind us that you are our refuge and our strength.

Teach us, Lord, how to love.
so that people observe our congregational life and say,
"See how they love each other."
Teach us how to love
so that we care equally about our sisters nearby and our brothers far away.
Teach us how to love
across denominational boundaries and political boundaries.

Teach us Lord,
how to be peacemakers in the face of militarism,
how to serve you with our heart, our mind, our soul, our body, our strength, our
income, and our time.
Give youth the strength to resist the call to become members of the military.
Give adults the strength to take the next risky step on the journey to be faithful
to you.
Teach us not to be shy, but to boldly say no to violence and yes to you.
Give us a nonresistant revival!

And teach us, Lord, to always keep you, our Lord and Savior, at the heart of our
peace work.

Now to God who by the power at work within us is able to accomplish abundantly far more than all we can ask or imagine, to God be glory in the church
and in Christ Jesus to all generations forever and ever (Ephesians 3:20-21).

Amen—Go now in peace.

—Susan Mark Landis

April 21

Mustard seeds matter

The apostles said to the Lord, "Increase our faith!" He replied,
"If you have faith as small as a mustard seed, you can say to this mulberry tree,
'Be uprooted and planted in the sea,' and it will obey you."

—Luke 17: 5-6 (NIV)

In this passage, we read of the disciples beseeching Jesus to increase their faith. Perhaps this is a cry or prayer you may have said at one time or another: "Lord, increase our faith! Help us believe enough so that we can do what it is that you have commanded us to do. Help us to trust enough so that we can live as you say we should be living. Lord, take away our fear!"

There is a tale about a traveler making his way to a large city. One night he meets two other travelers along the road—Fear and Plague.

Plague explains to the traveler that, once they arrive, they are expected to kill 10,000 people in the city. The traveler asks Plague if Plague would do all the killing. "Oh no," Plague responds. "I shall kill only a few hundred. My friend Fear will kill the others."

Fear, whether real or imagined, can discourage us, overwhelm us, and strangle us. Fear is widespread, ranging from fear of failure to fear of war and terrorists.

The disciples experienced many of these same feelings. In Luke 17:5-10, we read of their beseeching Jesus to increase their faith. Perhaps this is a cry or prayer you may have said at one time or another, "Lord, increase our faith! Help us believe enough so that we can do what it is that you have commanded us to do—help us to trust enough so that we can live as you say we should be living. Lord, take away our fear!"

How does Jesus respond to their pleas? Does he lay his hands on them and pray and give them more faith as they asked? Does he snap his fingers and grant them a double dose of the Holy Spirit? No. Instead, he says to them: "If you had faith the size of a mustard seed, you could say to this mulberry, 'Be uprooted and planted in the sea,' and it would obey you."

I think Jesus' odd response to the disciples can be explained through the concept of "the butterfly effect," the notion in chaos theory that no matter how complex a system is, the slightest change in initial conditions can have far-reaching effects, changing a system dynamically. Edward Lorenz first observed and proposed this theory in the 1960s when he was running computer models of weather measurements. When he entered even the slightest difference in the initial number in his equations, resulting outcomes were dramatically changed. His paper submitted for a scientific talk he gave in 1992 was titled, "Predictability: Does the Flap of a Butterfly's Wings in Brazil set off a Tornado in Texas?"

Might there be something in the butterfly effect that Jesus is trying to tell us? Is it possible that even the smallest intention and action toward following Jesus, toward doing the good, even the smallest glimpses of that holiness and wholeness in the midst of our fear and brokenness can help bring the kingdom of God into being?

In the novel and film *To Kill a Mockingbird*, the character Tom, an African-American, is wrongly accused of assaulting a white teenage girl and is held in the town jail. A group of white men approach the jail with the intention to lynch

Judith Baer Kulp

and kill Tom. On the front steps sits Tom's lawyer, Atticus Finch, the moral center of the novel. Atticus' daughter, Scout, runs to Atticus' side and she watches the men. Her father tells her to run away and go home. But Scout doesn't run, and she doesn't fight. Instead she finds the right words that become a kind of mustard seed.

Scout looks at one of the men in the mob and says, "Hey Mr. Cunningham, don't you remember me? I go to school with Walter. He's your boy, ain't he? We brought him home for dinner one time. Tell your boy 'hey' for me, will you?" There is a long pause. Then Cunningham responds to Scout: "I'll tell him you said 'Hey,' little lady," and he turns to leave.

With Cunningham's departure, the rest of the mob begins to break up and leave. Scout offered a small, gentle reminder of God's goodness. And what she said was a mustard seed—nothing courageous and noble—because she saw Mr. Cunningham's humanity and touched that humanity enough to bring him out of his irrational inhumanity. It was a "butterfly effect," a tiny mustard seed that changed the events of that night.

I am reminded of the prayer attributed to Francis of Assisi:

Lord, make me an instrument of thy peace;
where there is hatred, let me sow love;
where there is injury, pardon;
where there is doubt, faith;
where there is despair, hope;
where there is darkness, light;
and where there is sadness, joy…

In this world where doubt, hatred, and despair reign so supreme, it seems almost impossible that such small seeds of faith, love, and hope have much chance of surviving.

No wonder we cry out with the disciples, "Increase our faith!"

Remember that the slightest change in initial conditions, no matter how complex, can have far-reaching effects.

Mustard seeds matter.

—June Mears Driedger

J. Daryl Byler

Cedars of Lebanon

In Revelation 21, John sees a new heaven, a new earth, and the new Jerusalem. "See, I am making all things new," God declares. In this new order, God will dwell among humans, and there will be no more mourning, crying, or pain.

In the present moment, too often filled with suffering, violence, confusion, and disorder, it is sometimes hard to see the new things that God is creating. Still, as we are faithful to tend the trees by loving one another and accepting those who are different from us, God is faithful to look after the forest.

—J. Daryl Byler

Two salads — one vinaigrette

Shredded carrot salad with lemon juice vinaigrette

- shredded or grated carrots
- finely chopped parsley

Shred any amount of carrots. I do a pound for a potluck dish. For a pound of carrots, add a handful of parsley and toss to distribute.
Whisk vinaigrette and pour a small amount over carrots and toss.
Let stand for a few minutes before tasting and deciding to add more dressing, or just more lemon juice, salt, and pepper.

Spring wheat berry salad

- soft wheat berries
- any lettuce
- assorted spring vegetables
- toasted nuts

Rinse any amount of wheat berries in cold water and add to a generous amount of salted, boiling water. Simmer until cooked through, but still chewy, 45 minutes to an hour. Drain, pour into bowl, add a small amount of vinaigrette and toss thoroughly. When wheat berries have cooled, add lettuce (I like arugula – about a handful for every cup of uncooked berries) and any assorted spring vegetables like peas, blanched asparagus, shredded carrots and scallions. For a hearty main dish, add cooked, shredded chicken. Just before serving, sprinkle toasted nuts on top.

Lemon juice vinaigrette

1/2 cup fresh lemon juice
1/2 - 3/4 cup olive oil
salt & pepper

Start by adding a nice big pinch of salt to the lemon juice, whisking to dissolve. Still whisking, begin adding oil in a slow, steady stream. When you've added 1/2 cup of oil, taste. If it's too acidic, add more oil until it tastes bright but balanced. Add fresh pepper to taste. In addition to the two salads mentioned here, it's wonderful on fresh greens.

—Audrey Hindes DiPalma

54

April 22

Earth Day: Nourishing body and community

...O God... You visit the earth and water it, you greatly enrich it; the river of God is full of water; you provide the people with grain, for so you have prepared it. You water its furrows abundantly, settling its ridges, softening it with showers, and blessing its growth. You crown the year with your bounty; your wagon tracks overflow with richness. The pastures of the wilderness overflow, the hills gird themselves with joy, the meadows clothe themselves with flocks, the valleys deck themselves with grain, they shout and sing together for joy.

—Psalm 65:5-13 (NRSV)

With spring well on its way, now is the perfect time to get involved with Community Supported Agriculture (CSA). The main reason to join a CSA, as it's called, is to access freshly picked, locally grown produce, rather than to buy the usual fruits and vegetables trucked in from afar, which are often unripe and lack flavor. But by participating in the CSA, you'll not only be nourishing your own body. You'll also be caring for your community–a larger kind of body–by supporting small-scale farmers and local businesses. And you'll be fostering a healthy environment and soil, because most farms involved in CSA are organic or biodynamic, which means they apply little or no harmful pesticides and herbicides.

Another bonus is the culinary adventure. Unusual varieties of produce are often available through CSA. Vegetables like Cowhorn fingerling potatoes, banana peppers, Thai green peas, and Italian Annelino beans, as well as fruits like toad skin melons may grace your table. By growing nearly extinct heirloom varieties, small-scale farmers are also helping to preserve a bit of our past and safeguard our biodiversity.

CSA is especially attractive if you don't or can't have a large garden. However, if you are a farmer, you can gain from CSA on the sales end, as it provides an

Carol Penner

excellent outlet for marketing directly to consumers. Beyond that, participating in this international movement, which was launched in the 1960s by a group of Japanese women, also reduces our dependence on fossil fuels by minimizing delivery distances, which are typically quite far. A tomato, for example, usually travels about 1,300 miles from where it is grown to your salad bowl, according to the U.S. Department of Agriculture.

Here's how CSA works: You pay a fixed price at the beginning of the season for a "share" or "subscription" in a local farm. In return for your advance financing of labor and supplies, including everything from seeds to machinery, you receive a supply of herbs, veggies, fruits, and sometimes flowers as they become available, usually on a weekly basis. Some farms offer pick-your-own and delivery options, while all usually provide ways to visit and educate yourselves and children about the origins of food.

A little attitude adjustment may be required. After all, you have to organize your pocketbook to pay up front; you may get more or less than you desire, depending on the weather and management; you won't find the daily selection available at average grocery stores. But, no matter what, you'll be sharing an experience and a connection to the land that many feel is invaluable. And when you bite into those tasty heirloom tomatoes, sun-ripened berries or kale sweetened by the first frost, eating with the seasons will beat the grocery store any time.

For more information on CSA, or to find a CSA organization in your area, try the USDA's Alternative Farming Systems Information Center at http://www.nal. usda.gov/afsic/csa. This site has an amazing and extensive list of further info; be sure to note the "resources for farmers or producers" section, which is informative for consumers, too!

—*Kristi Bahrenburg Janzen*

Peace at home

It is not enemies who taunt me—I could bear that;
it is not adversaries who deal insolently with me—I could hide from them.
But it is you, my equal, my companion, my familiar friend,
with whom I kept pleasant company; we walked in the house of God with the throng.

—Psalm 55:12-14 (NRSV)

One of the grim realities of life in our society is the violence that occurs in our families and homes. An average of three or four women are murdered every day in the United States by their husbands or boyfriends. While this number has declined over the past few decades, it is still a higher average than the daily number of U.S. soldiers killed these past years in Iraq and Afghanistan.

Dating violence is also an increasing problem, with one in three adolescent girls experiencing physical, emotional, or verbal abuse from a dating partner, according to a report published by the Action Center of the Family Violence Prevention Fund.

According to Nancy Nason-Clark, author of *The Battered Wife* and other titles related to family violence, the incidence of abuse in Christian homes is similar to general society; the only difference is that Christian women tend to remain in an abusive relationship longer.

One woman described her experience this way:

"Whenever people share a living space they run into little problems…but in our house the problems would not be solved… I'd try harder to please him but he would not be soothed… physical and verbal abuse became a regular pattern. He would grab me or push me if he thought I wasn't listening to him. He would throw things, tell me that I was a lousy wife or mother or housekeeper.

"A beating is a hard thing to describe. It's a hard thing to remember, not because the memories have faded, but because they are so clear and painful. I felt an inexpressible fear, my arms pinned immobile to a bed by the knees of the man I loved, his fist coming toward my face.

"I have looked in the mirror and not recognized myself.

"I finally realized that I was living in a kind of hell, and that it surely couldn't be God's will for anyone to live like this. So I ran away to the Crisis Intervention Center in my town. That's where I began to learn to be alive again" (excerpted from a story at: http://abuse.mcc.org).

The consequences of such violence are severe, not only emotionally, physically, and spiritually, but also in terms of major disease. For instance, women who have experienced domestic violence are 80 percent more likely to have a stroke, 70 percent more likely to have heart disease, 60 percent more likely to have asthma, and 70 percent more likely to drink heavily than women who have not experienced intimate partner violence, according to a Centers for Disease Control and Prevention report in 2008.

As Christians who seek to follow Jesus' way of peace, these realities challenge us. What do we say? What do we teach? How do we support those experiencing abuse? How do we confront and hold accountable those who behave abusively? How do we work at prevention?

—*Linda Gehman Peachey*

Action steps

For discussion and reflection

1. Who in your community addresses domestic violence? What additional efforts are needed? To whom should I talk about volunteering?
2. How does your congregation address violence in the home? What additional steps could be taken? One easy step is to post helpline information in the privacy of restroom stalls.

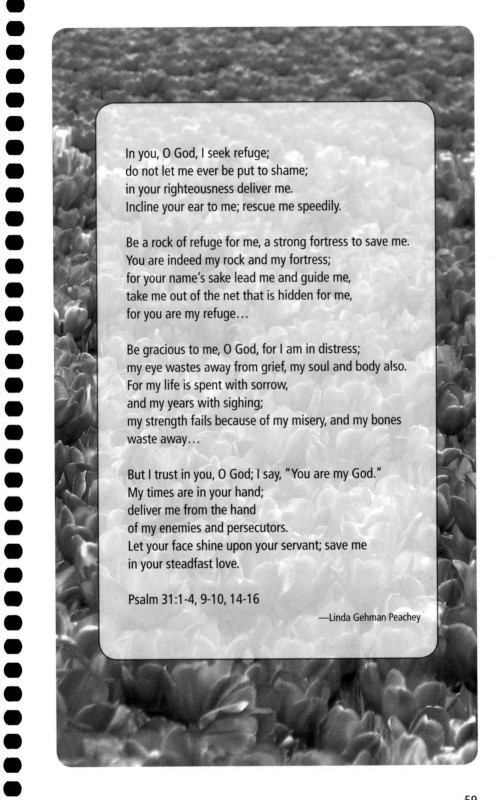

In you, O God, I seek refuge;
do not let me ever be put to shame;
in your righteousness deliver me.
Incline your ear to me; rescue me speedily.

Be a rock of refuge for me, a strong fortress to save me.
You are indeed my rock and my fortress;
for your name's sake lead me and guide me,
take me out of the net that is hidden for me,
for you are my refuge…

Be gracious to me, O God, for I am in distress;
my eye wastes away from grief, my soul and body also.
For my life is spent with sorrow,
and my years with sighing;
my strength fails because of my misery, and my bones
waste away…

But I trust in you, O God; I say, "You are my God."
My times are in your hand;
deliver me from the hand
of my enemies and persecutors.
Let your face shine upon your servant; save me
in your steadfast love.

Psalm 31:1-4, 9-10, 14-16

—Linda Gehman Peachey

Peace is not controlling

"'Which of these three, do you think, was a neighbor to the man who fell into the hands of the robbers?' He said, 'The one who showed him mercy.' Jesus said to him, 'Go and do likewise.'"

—Luke 10:25-37 (NRSV)

A m I my brother's keeper?

No, I am my brother's brother.

Jesus told the story of the Good Samaritan (Luke 10:25-37) to answer a lawyer who wanted to know: "Who is my neighbor?" At the conclusion of the story, instead of saying, "Now do you understand who is your neighbor?" Jesus asked the lawyer, "Which man was the neighbor?" The latter does not permit judgment of others, or self-oriented selectivity. Rather, the question is whether we are willing to be neighborly.

This spirit of neighborliness could transform the world. Think of what it could mean to have a world neighborhood in which we shared with those in need—where we worked on an economy of development rather than supporting economies by militarism. Think of what it would mean in the Middle East if the Israelis and the Palestinians could become good neighbors to each other. Think of the implications for America's foreign policy if we sought to be neighborly rather than to give every indication that we are a controlling power. We will not enable peace between peoples by seeking to control them.

Imperialism is not the answer to relationships in the global community. No one nation has the right or authority to control others. It is far better to share for the enrichment of others, to engage the dialogue that demonstrates social and political values of freedom, so that this becomes the quest of all peoples. This we need to promote in our own context and let it attract others.

Within each of us is a resistance to being controlled by another. Recognizing this as a human characteristic gives a spirit and a pattern for service. Service is meeting another at their point of need. True service means to serve others in the way in which they need to be served, not in the way in which we determine to serve them. The latter would mean that we are still in charge.

One with the spirit of a servant can go anywhere in the world and relate without threatening others. Jesus came "not to be ministered unto but to minister, to serve, and to give his life a ransom for many." The great Christological passage of Philippians 2 presents Jesus as the Son/Servant of God, who became the servant of humanity. Paul entreats us that this same mind is to characterize the life of the believer.

—Myron Augsburger

Courtesy of Carol Rose

"He that planteth a tree is a servant of God, he provideth a kindness for many generations, and faces that he hath not seen shall bless him."

—Henry Van Dyke

Defeating the forces of domination and death

When he came to Nazareth, where he had been brought up,
he went to the synagogue on the sabbath day, as was his custom.
He stood up to read, and the scroll of the prophet Isaiah was given to him.
He unrolled the scroll and found the place where it was written:
"The Spirit of the Lord is upon me,
because he has anointed me to bring good news to the poor.
He has sent me to proclaim release to the captives and recovery of sight to the blind,
to let the oppressed go free,
to proclaim the year of the Lord's favor."

—Luke 4:16-19 (NRSV)

When individuals and nations are determined to behave as conquerors and dominators instead of as neighbors, I wonder how Christians should respond. I believe the answer lies in faith-based nonviolent direct action, a "getting in the way," as the Christian Peacemaker Teams motto states, of those who embrace violence and domination.

This type of resistance has taken many forms. For example, Austrian farmer Franz Jaegerstaetter believed God told him in a dream that he must not join the army of the Third Reich. Despite intense pressure from the Catholic Church hierarchy, Jaegerstaetter remained resolute. The Nazis beheaded him in 1943 for conscientious objection.

Christians involved with the civil rights movement in the southern United States in the 1950s and '60s sang and prayed when white racists arrested and assaulted them. In 1997, paramilitaries slaughtered men, women, and children belonging to a group of pacifist Christian Mayan Indians called Las Abejas (the Bees) as they prayed in the Acteal refugee camp in Chiapas, Mexico. Despite the fact that the Mexican military had allowed the paramilitaries inside the camp and prevented other refugees in the adjacent Zapatista camp from helping the victims, Las Abejas invited Mexican soldiers to join their prayer vigils in the following months as they protested the militarization of their region.

Faith-based nonviolent direct action also allows its practitioners to witness for Christ. It gives Christians a chance to say to the disenfranchised, "I am standing with you because I follow Jesus, who advocated for the powerless." It enables them to tell those who hate them, "Despite what you do to me, you cannot make me hate you, because I follow Jesus, who told us to love our enemies."

Orthodox Archbishop Anastasios of Albania exemplified this Christian witness when he organized relief efforts to assist the predominantly Muslim refugees from Kosovo fleeing Serb soldiers and paramilitaries in 1999. "We were tempted to stay on the sideline in prayer," he said, "but then, that would not be authentic, since we are obliged to see in the faces of the suffering people the face of Christ." For this witness to Christ's love, he became almost as revered by Albanian Muslims as he was by Albanian Christians.

I have personally experienced the ways that nonviolent direct action becomes a Christian witness as a result of my work in Hebron with Christian Peacemaker Teams. Palestinian Christians have told CPT that they used to be afraid of going to Hebron, but no longer feel that way, because now when the devout and pugnacious Muslim residents of Hebron think of Christians, they will think of CPT.

I think faith-based nonviolent direct action also helps allay bitterness when the hard work for reconciliation and justice is turned into dust by the forces of domination. As Christians, we can take the long view of history and remember that Jesus' followers in the first century believed he would return and establish the Kingdom of God in their lifetimes. Even though Jesus did not return in the first century, we still live in hope of his coming again. We know that the Kingdom continues despite the efforts of lesser powers and principalities to destroy it.

Though in the short term our efforts may seem to fail, Jesus has already defeated the forces of domination and death. Our actions in behalf of the suffering in the present are simply characteristic of those who belong to the Kingdom of God, where being a good citizen means being a good neighbor.

—*Kathleen Kern*

The foreseeable future

By the tender mercy of our God,
the dawn from on high will break upon us,
to give light to those who sit in darkness and in the shadow of death,
to guide our feet into the way of peace.

—Luke 1:78 (NRSV)

A hymn of praise for fists uncurled!
Alleluias on our lips for ammunition abandoned!
Guns dropped, forgotten,
bombs defused, harmless!
Fervent thanks for tanks rusting,
for jet fighters permanently grounded!
This future, peace-bright,
hovers on the horizon of your kingdom.
It will dawn the day we remember
there are no soldiers—
    only your children, beloved and loving,
there are no borders—
    only one world, creative and creating,
there has been no collateral damage—
    only broken hearts, broken homes, broken dreams.
It will come the day we remember to pray,
"Your kingdom come, your will be done."
The Spirit and the church say, "Come!"

—*Carol Penner*

Carol Penner

"In the spring,
at the end of the day,
you should smell like dirt."

—Margaret Atwood

April 27

Justice and peace

"Take away from me the noise of your songs;
I will not even listen to the sound of your harps. But let justice roll down like waters
and righteousness like an ever-flowing stream."

—Amos 5:23-24 (NRSV)

Reestablishing the peace that existed in creation is God's ultimate objective. This peace is the peace of shalom. Perry Yoder describes shalom as material prosperity for all; healthy, right relationships; and moral integrity. It is a holistic, all-encompassing well-being throughout all of creation.

Justice is a kind of litmus test for any situation to see if shalom truly exists. Things may be calm, quiet, and apparently "peaceful"; however, if there is injustice, peace does not truly exist. If some prosper while others do not, possibly even at the expense of others, there is not shalom. If war is used to rescue an oppressed people, then there is not shalom since enemies are hated, harmed or killed; innocent people may also be harmed or killed; the earth is ravaged by weapons; and God's commandment, "You shall not kill" is broken. For peace to truly exist, there must be justice.

A shorter version of Yoder's definition of peace is that shalom is when "things are as they ought to be." Things are not as they ought to be when some prosper and others do not; when some cause harm or death, when some deny rights to others, or when some must work long hours for little pay so that others can buy expensive goods. While in each of these cases there may not be open conflict, nevertheless, there is not shalom.

Seeing justice as that which maintains or establishes "things as they ought to be" views justice differently from our traditional idea of justice derived from Greek and Roman philosophy. Rather than being seen as what is deserved, either positively or negatively, God's justice is seen as that which is needed. Rather than punishment or reward, God's justice delivers justice that redeems, restores, reconciles.

So, as peacemakers seeking to establish and maintain the holistic peace of shalom, we must do more than avoid violence and conflict. We must seek to promote and maintain justice.

—*Tom Beutel*

"Worrying is less work than doing something. Everybody wants to save the earth; nobody wants to help Mom with the dishes."

—P.J. O'Rourke

Action steps

For justice

1. Cut your use of waste and energy. Give your savings to a relief organization to supply food, water, heat, or education to people without enough.
2. Examine your budget to see how you can switch some purchases, such as coffee and tea, to fairly traded products.

For the sake of the gospel

I do it all for the sake of the gospel.

—1 Corinthians 9:23 (NRSV)

The Meserete Kristos Church in Ethiopia is the largest body of Mennonites in the world. Years ago, when the former government restricted the Christian church, the church went underground and grew by leaps and bounds. Now the government is more open and the church continues to grow.

Sunday morning I visited the largest Meserete Kristos church in Addis Ababa with about 50 others who were in the city for a service consultation. Arli Klassen, Mennonite Central Committee executive director, shared with the congregation of 2,000 that Glen Lapp, MCC service worker in Afghanistan, had been killed along with others who worked for International Assistance Missions (AIM).

Even though we can't see, we have hope, the preacher told the congregation. Glen's faith in God gave him the courage to sacrifice himself for others. Faith is not denying things, the pastor told us, it is about believing that God can change things.

The preacher's words were sobering to the Mennonite and Brethren in Christ leaders who had gathered to talk about how we can better serve the church and serve the world. Service is not just a concept, it's the way we are called to live.

Glen Lapp's death is a reminder to all of us that following Christ, serving others, can be costly. But that is what we are called to do. God can change things, in that we have hope, and we are called to serve.

In one of his last reports to MCC about his work in Afghanistan, Glen said that his hope was that he could treat people with respect and with love and try to be a little bit of Christ in this part of the world. In his life and in his death Glen demonstrated his love for others.

"May our worship please you," the choirs sang on Sunday morning. "Your mercy is so big and your love draws us to you," their song continued.

Later in the church service, an elder told us that we owe God everything. Glen Lapp showed us that sometimes that includes our lives.

Glen's death gave meaning to the banner which hung above the sanctuary on this Sunday morning: "I do it all for the sake of the gospel."

—Ron Byler

A girl harvests vegetables from a community garden
funded through Canadian Foodgrains Bank, a partnership of
Canadian churches and church-based agencies working to end
hunger in developing countries.

April 29

Our groans

Our groans

Creator God, our groans are your groans

Creator God, we groan with what the world experiences regarding
migration and movement of people across national borders. Often
we do not understand what this means.

Creator God, we groan because we do not know how to best
respond to the stranger, the refugee, the immigrant, and the
displaced who often walk from one land to another land or who walk
daily into our lives. We groan because we do not always know how to
participate in your Kingdom-building work here on earth.

Creator God, as we groan may we remember to pray for your
children around the world who experience migration troubles. May we
remember to pray for your children who experience violence and
destruction. May we remember that your arms extend to all.

Creator God, as we shed our tears help us understand what you ask of
us as your children arrive in our communities. May we see each other's
tears as signs of love and solidarity with those who experience
uncertainty and anxiety. May we remember that our tears help us
understand that we too are strangers in this land.

Creator God, in our groans I pray that we will remember to trust the
Spirit in all of what is happening in the world and in our local
communities regarding welcoming your children. May we remember
that your Spirit prays for us when we reach the end of words. May we
remember that we are never prayerless.

Creator God, may we find in our times of silence your wisdom to
know how to best participate in your Kingdom-building work with the
oppressed, the stranger, the refugee, the immigrant, the displaced, and
the downtrodden.

Creator God, may we remember that our groans are your groans.

Amen.

—Gilberto Pérez, Jr.

*I have surely seen the mistreatment of my people who are in Egypt
and have heard their groaning,
and I have come down to rescue them.*
—Acts 7:34 (NRSV)

Nuestro dolor

Dios, creador, nuestro dolor es tu dolor

Dios, creador, nuestro dolor es a causa de lo que el mundo
experimenta en cuanto al movimiento de personas a través de
fronteras nacionales. Reconocemos que muchas veces no
entendemos el significado de todo esto.

Dios, creador, tenemos dolor por que a veces no sabemos como
responder al extranjero, al refugiado, al inmigrante, y al desplazado
que camina de un país a otro o que llega a nuestras vidas. Tenemos
dolor porque no siempre sabemos como participar en tu reino aquí en
este mundo.

Dios, creador, al sentir nuestro dolor ayúdanos a orar por tus hijos
alrededor del mundo que tienen dificultades con asuntos de migración.
Que siempre recordemos orar por tus hijos que experimentan
violencia y destrucción. Que siempre recordemos que tus brazos se
extienden a todos los seres humanos.

Dios, creador, al nosotros derramar nuestras lágrimas ayúdanos a
entender lo que pides de nosotros cuando tus hijos llegan a nuestras
comunidades. Que nuestras lágrimas sean una señal de amor y
solidaridad con aquellos que experimentan incertidumbre y ansiedad.
Que podamos recordar que nuestras lágrimas nos ayudan a entender
que nosotros también somos extranjeros en esta tierra.

Dios, creador, en nuestro dolor oro que recordemos confiar en el
Espíritu en todo lo que sucede en el mundo respecto a darles la
bienvenida a tus hijos. Que siempre recordemos que cuando no
tengamos palabras tu Espíritu ora por nosotros.

Dios, creador, te pido que encontremos sabiduría en nuestros
momentos de silencio y que sepamos como responder al trabajo de tu
reino con el oprimido, el extranjero, el refugiado, el inmigrante y el desplazado.

Dios, creador, que siempre recordemos que nuestro dolor es tu dolor.

—Gilberto Pérez, Jr.

April 30

God will take care of me

When I look at your heavens, the work of your fingers,
the moon and the stars that you have established;
what are human beings that you are mindful of them,
mortals that you care for them?

—Psalm 8:3-4 (NRSV)

I learned to know Maria, an undocumented Mexican immigrant, when I volunteered in our adult education program in the early 1980s. She came to town because she heard there was work. She hadn't found any, but she had found Marta and José, generous people who invited Maria and her toddler son to live in their teeny house with them and their children.

I taught Maria and Marta English. José supported his family and Maria with his thriving truck mechanics business. Maria's son, whose father was a U. S. citizen, and who was born after a quick border crossing into the United States, received WIC and some rent assistance, which somehow was legal for Maria to use as his mother and caretaker. The legal situation didn't make sense to me, but that didn't matter. I was just the English tutor.

Until one day Maria called to ask me to take her to the bus station. She was mad at Marta and José and was leaving to live with a cousin in Chicago. I agreed to come over for a talk. When I understood that Maria hadn't heard from her cousin in over three years, I suggested we try to contact her and that Maria and her toddler live with Dennis, my husband, and me for a bit. Knowing how transient Maria was, I was afraid Maria's cousin had moved, leaving Maria stranded in Chicago without a place to stay. I also hoped to repair what had been a good relationship between Marta and Maria.

Over the next few days Maria's anxiety grew. She wasn't comfortable in our home, afraid her toddler would break something. We talked at length, encouraging her to stay with us where it was warm and dry, until she had someone to welcome them. "What will you do if your cousin has moved? Where will you live? How will you stay warm?" we asked as we offered unsolicited advice. Her answer was always the same, "If she isn't there, God will find someone else to care for us." We thought we were strong God-believers, but that Maria's thinking was naive.

When we got up Sunday morning, Maria was adamant that she would leave. I reluctantly helped her gather things together, adding sweaters and cash to as many disposable diapers as she could carry. I searched the house for something to stash it all in and found a Mennonite Central Committee grocery bag. I turned it over and saw the MCC logo and a light went on! I filled it up, handed it to Maria, and said, "When you get off the bus in Chicago, have this side of the bag showing." "Why?" she was puzzled. "I don't know," I admitted.

We put Maria and her son on the bus and I spent the rest of the day phoning people in Chicago. Finally I reached Paul Weaver, a friend who was working with refugees fleeing the Central American wars.

"That bus station will be swarming with immigration officers who will throw her and the boy in prison while they sort out the situation," he explained. "I'd better meet her. How will I know who she is?" "I don't believe it," I stuttered, "but she's carrying an MCC bag."

Paul scooped Maria up at the bus station before she had a chance to look confused and be arrested by the immigration agents. He drove her to the cousin's apartment. She no longer lived there and no one on the floor had ever heard of her. Maria stayed in Paul's household for a while until she reached her son's father—who I sensed abused her—and went to live with him. We wrote for a while. After a bit she stopped writing, possibly because I wouldn't pay the shipping costs for her son's large, cheap plastic toys to California or because I kept telling her that she didn't deserve to be beaten.

Maria taught me a great deal. Through her eyes I learned what little sense invisible lines on the ground make to some people. She was born in Mexico almost within sight of the border with the United States. She believed her life and opportunities would have been immeasurably different if she had been born "just over there" and that her poverty was a quirk of fate. Border laws made little sense; national sovereignty wasn't a part of her vocabulary. The transience that terrified me was her way of life. I also realized that I didn't have a right to advise Maria how to live, that my middle-class sensibilities didn't work in her world, and that I couldn't fix her layers of problems.

As I've worked on immigration issues recently, the Good Samaritan parable has given me new insights. I notice the Good Samaritan did only so much for the man along the road. He didn't make the road safe for the next man to walk along, he didn't rehabilitate the robbers, he didn't even ensure economic stability for the man after he was healed. However, Jesus did hold the Good Samaritan responsible to do what needed doing in the moment, when he found the wounded man and paid for his care out of his own pocket.

Immigration laws are a huge mess in the United States; everyone agrees about that. There are no easy answers, and likely there aren't even hard answers that are just or will solve many of the problems. That doesn't let us Christians off the hook, however. We are still responsible for the people in our neighborhoods, working to ensure they have the quality of life God desires for them. And we are responsible to encourage our government to be as just as possible. That's the responsibility of citizens in a democracy. The economic inequalities between the sides of the border aren't going to be solved by a fence or a patrol. Someone recently told me he didn't want to hear a sermon about immigration, "Because that's where Christian rubber really hits the road. Immigration problems are mostly caused by unequal distribution of income." I wonder, if the United States spent the billions we will use in building the fence on rebuilding economies we've destroyed, might fewer people desire to live here, and might we be safer?

After Maria was safely settled, I said to my husband one night, "You know, Maria was right: God did take care of her."

"Yeah," he replied. "But God's people sure had to work hard."

—Susan Mark Landis

Otterville   Merrill R. Miller

Celebrate God's gift of vegetables: Black bean & onion relish

Praise the Lord, my soul. Lord my God, you are very great;
you are clothed with splendor and majesty.
He makes…plants for people to cultivate—
bringing forth food from the earth:
wine that gladdens human hearts, oil to make their faces shine,
and bread that sustains their hearts.

—Psalm 104

Black bean and onion relish is a wonderful dish. I love to make it! Hand slicing, dicing, and chopping the vegetables is a process that is contemplative for me. As I work, I often think of the people I will serve. There is something very pleasing about the contrasts in this recipe. There's the crunch of the fresh vegetables, and the soft consistency of the beans and hominy. I like the sweet and sour tastes. The variety of textures, colors, and flavors of this dish make it a delight for the eye and palate! I always make sure to serve it in a large clear bowl to show off the colors.

Part of the enjoyment of cooking is watching people eat the food I prepare. Often I hear people try to identify the vegetables. When I serve it with crispy tortilla chips, it gets raves, and I get requests for the recipe.

Black bean and onion relish
Combine and heat 1/2 cup vinegar and 1/2 cup oil to dissolve 1/2 cup sugar.
1 can (15 ounce) black beans
1 can (15 ounce) white hominy, rinsed
1 can petite diced tomatoes, drained (or 2 tomatoes, chopped)
1 teaspoon salt
1/4 teaspoon ground pepper
2 garlic cloves, pressed or minced
4 green onions, finely sliced
1 small onion, finely chopped
1 small green pepper, finely chopped
1/2 cup celery, chopped
Mix all vegetables together and combine with cooled vinegar-oil-sugar mixture. Refrigerate for several hours. Serve with tortilla chips.

—Carol Honderich

J. Daryl Byler

Holy Week

Palm Sunday

*The next day the great crowd that had come for the festival heard that
Jesus was on his way to Jerusalem. They took palm branches and
went out to meet him, shouting, "Hosanna!"*
"Blessed is he who comes in the name of the Lord!"
"Blessed is the king of Israel!"
Jesus found a young donkey and sat on it, as it is written:
"Do not be afraid, Daughter Zion;
see, your king is coming, seated on a donkey's colt."
At first his disciples did not understand all this.
*Only after Jesus was glorified did they realize that these things had been written
about him and that these things had been done to him.*

—John 12: 12-16 (NIV)

I work in a state-funded program that assists mentally ill adults who have
wound up homeless or in jail. As a frontline worker, I pick up our clients from jails or psychiatric hospitals, secure food and housing for them,
arrange mental health treatment to stabilize them, help them learn independent
living skills, and manage crises as they arise. I find my work to be rewarding,
sometimes fun.

Despite all of the work and the responsibility, we frontline workers occupy
a fairly low position in the agency hierarchy. Our low pay and lack of authority reflect our humble status. Managerial staff earn from two to 15 times more.
They also have more power, drive fancier cars, and live in larger homes in more
affluent neighborhoods.

When I was in my 20s, being at the bottom of this sort of hierarchy did
not bother me much. Now in my mid-40s, my humble status has, surprisingly,
begun to affect my self-esteem. Although I never wanted to climb the proverbial
ladder of success and always kept professionalism and careerism at arm's length,
choosing instead to focus on simplicity, community and faith, I still find myself
pondering the mystery of how I ended up in such a mean estate in the world of
paid work. Did I fail? Did I not work hard enough? Did I refuse to grow up?

When these questions become oppressive, I take comfort in the gospel, a
story about a working class Messiah who found his home among the common
poor and the outcasts of society. Jesus preached a gospel that was understood by

"little children" (Mark 10:14) and "infants" (Matthew 11:25) and rejected by the "wise" (Matthew 11:25) and the powerful.

The Palm Sunday story epitomizes the power that Jesus exercised through what the world calls weakness. Whereas imperial dignitaries would enter Jerusalem with warhorses and chariots in a grand display of power and glory, Jesus entered riding a simple donkey, a worker animal. The people hailed him king and his first act as king was to wash other people's feet (John 13:3-5).

Reflecting on the gospel, I think that Jesus of Nazareth would approve of my work and where I've ended up. I don't drive a fancy car, and I live in a poor neighborhood, but I think it is easier to find God here.

—Bert Newton

Palm Sunday Peace Parade

In Pasadena, California, our understanding of the Palm Sunday story forms the basis for our peace parade.

On the first Palm Sunday, Jesus culminated his journey from the margins of his society, Galilee, to the center, Jerusalem. The common people triumphantly waved Jesus into Jerusalem as their chosen king. There in Jerusalem he confronted the powers that oppressed the people when he went to the Temple and shut it down (Mark 11:16) and continued to preach in parables against the ruling establishment.

We gather in a church in the economically marginalized part of our city, where some of us live. We sing and introduce the various congregations and community groups in attendance. We hear a brief inspirational explanation of our parade and the historical, biblical account of the first parade in Jerusalem. Then we bless the parade with a prayer and march out onto the sidewalk.

We march with palm branches, signs, peace flags, drums, and other instruments less than a mile to an upscale mall that represents the economic center of the city. This mall is a symbolic temple which represents the consumerism that funds wars through an oppressive economic system.

Because the mall does not allow us onto their property, we we gather in a wide place on the sidewalk where we have set up a sound system. Having marched from the economic margins to the economic center of our community, we *confront* the principalities and powers with songs, prayers, and gospel proclamation.

The parade is a family friendly celebration.

I share our experience in Pasadena as one way to inspire and encourage even more creative expressions of the Palm Sunday peace parade.

—Bert Newton

79

Holy Week

Monday

Holy resistance: A Holy Week tradition

Now Cain said to his brother Abel, "Let's go out to the field." While they were in the field, Cain attacked his brother Abel and killed him. Then the Lord said to Cain, "Where is your brother Abel?" "I don't know," he replied. "Am I my brother's keeper?" The Lord said, "What have you done? Listen! Your brother's blood cries out to me from the ground."

—Genesis 4:8-10

And Mary said: "My soul glorifies the Lord and my spirit rejoices in God my Savior, for he has been mindful of the humble state of his servant. From now on all generations will call me blessed, for the Mighty One has done great things for me—holy is his name. His mercy extends to those who fear him, from generation to generation. He has performed mighty deeds with his arm; he has scattered those who are proud in their inmost thoughts. He has brought down rulers from their thrones but has lifted up the humble. He has filled the hungry with good things but has sent the rich away empty. He has helped his servant Israel, remembering to be merciful to Abraham and his descendants forever, just as he promised our ancestors."

—Luke 1:46-55

On Good Friday, 1963, Martin Luther King, Jr. and Ralph Abernathy left the Sixteenth Street Baptist Church a few hours after the announced starting time for the march. They led nearly forty people who were willing to be arrested by the notorious Bull Connor, sheriff of Birmingham, Alabama. But according to Taylor Branch in his book, *Parting the Waters*, the midday crowds of African-Americans stood along the expected route, talking excitedly about whether King and Abernathy would face the infamous Connor. "The long-awaited first sight of King touched off shouts of celebration and encouragement, which grew louder as the marchers pushed their way down the sidewalks for several blocks." By the time the line reached the police blockade, reported in the next morning's The New York Times, "More than a thousand shouting, singing Negroes had joined in the demonstration."

When King made an unexpected turn, the police pulled U-turns in pursuit with reporters and white pedestrians following them. When the line of police re-formed across King's path, "the pageantry of confrontation played out abruptly," writes Branch. Without warning, a detective seized King by the back of his belt, lifted him off the ground and shoved him into a paddy wagon. Another officer pushed Abernathy in the same direction. Eventually 52 people were jailed with King and Abernathy. Bull Connor told reporters that King was getting what he wanted.

At the jail, Connor had the police separate King from everyone else and refused King's request to make phone calls or talk with his lawyers. King was placed into solitary confinement. According to Branch, on Easter Monday, King was moved out of solitary confinement to a cell with other prisoners and his visitation rights were restored. He read in The Birmingham News the headline, "White Clergymen Urge Local Negroes to Withdraw from Demonstrations." After attacking the Birmingham demonstrations as "unwise and untimely," and commending the news media and the police for "the calm manner in which these demonstrations have been handled," the clergymen invoked their religious authority against civil disobedience.

In response, King wrote his famous "Letter from a Birmingham Jail," addressed to his clergy colleagues. "I must make two honest confessions to you, my Christian and Jewish brothers. First, I must confess that over the last few years I have been gravely disappointed with the white moderate. I have almost reached the regrettable conclusion that the Negro's great stumbling block is not the White Citizen's Council-er or the Ku Klux Klanner, but the white moderate who is more devoted to 'order' than to justice, who prefers a negative peace which is the absence of tension to a positive peace which is the presence of justice, who constantly says, 'I agree with you in the goal you seek, but I can't agree with your methods of direct action,' who paternalistically believes that he can set the timetable for another man's freedom…," he said.

This week is Holy Week in the Christian church calendar. Jesus' action on Palm Sunday was the crux of his strategy to bring himself and his message to Jerusalem. This was not a big public relations thrust or an evangelistic effort because of the large number of people in Jerusalem for Passover. Rather, Jesus' parade into Jerusalem reflected the Jewish people's vision that God would bring about a change beginning with Jerusalem. For Jesus, to affirm the vision of the kingdom of God and to live out its hopes through action and symbol meant challenging the existing structures of authority, both in the established religious leadership and in the Roman leadership. The significance of Jesus' Palm Sunday journey for us means challenging the powers that hold sway both in our world and in our churches.

In March 1980, another prophet of God was killed while performing mass in El Salvador. In the three years that Oscar Romero served as Archbishop of El Salvador, Romero moved from a mild-mannered priest, who was initially described as "unobtrusive and willing to toe the line" by his contemporaries, to a fiery prophet of God, considered so dangerous by the ruling powers that he had to be assassinated. He was considered dangerous because he began to speak the truth.

In his first pastoral letter to the Christians in El Salvador, Romero wrote, "The Church does not live for itself. Its reason for being is the same as that of Jesus: service to God in order to serve the world." The Church, he said, must make its own "the hopes and joys, the anxieties and sorrows" of human beings. The Church, like Jesus, is sent to bring good news to the poor, to lift up the downtrodden, to seek out and save the lost. The Church must therefore act like Jesus—it must resist and denounce all that opposes God's reign, all the injustice and callousness built into society, just as Jesus denounced the sins of his contemporaries and their society.

Romero said the Church thus faces the fundamental option of faith; to favor life or death. "With great clarity we see that in this no neutrality is possible. Either we serve the life of Salvadorans or we are accomplices in their death. It is the expression in history of what is most fundamental in the faith: either we believe in a God of life, or we serve the idols of death," he said.

We too are faced with the fundamental option of faith: to favor life or death. We too are faced with the question of what we will do with a Messiah who ushers in a reign of peace, not warfare. We too are faced with the question: will we be more devoted to orderliness or justice?

During Holy Week, I suggest the discipline of praying for God's kingdom to reign on earth just as it currently reigns in heaven. Let us follow Jesus this Holy Week and let us continue into the season of Pentecost.

—June Mears Driedger

Immigration rally in Washington, D.C.

Ryan Rodrick Beiler

Turning tables

Then Jesus entered the temple and drove out all who were selling and buying in the temple, and he overturned the tables of the money-changers and the seats of those who sold doves. He said to them, "It is written, 'My house shall be called a house of prayer'; but you are making it a den of robbers."

—Matthew 21:21 (NRSV)

Sunday school didn't go as any of us expected Palm Sunday and that's *good*! God is at work in my kindergarten-second grade students. Our Sunday school materials encouraged me to bring a cape and let the kids talk about their favorite superhero. Eventually I was to turn the conversation toward Jesus, who has the "real" superpowers.

But when I asked the kids who their favorite superhero was, they all said Jesus! Well, there went the introduction to the lesson. So they each tried on the big blue beach towel I had brought and skipped around being Jesus helping people. Oh, eventually some were Spiderman or Batman, but we all knew Jesus had this competition tied up right from the start. I later complimented the parents for teaching their children so well.

Then we talked about whether the kids would like to come to my house on Good Friday. My purpose was to give the kids an opportunity to hear about Jesus' last week. Our congregation doesn't have a Good Friday service or Sunday school on Easter. I didn't want my kids to be like one child sitting in church on Easter Sunday. The preacher said Jesus had risen from the dead and the child looked up at his mom in alarm. "I didn't even know Jesus was sick!"

When I asked the kids if they wanted to come to my house, they wondered if they could have a party. We talked some about what a party is and what Easter is. The youngest got a thoughtful look on his face. "Easter isn't about bunnies and eggs; it's about Jesus!"

We moved into our Bible story. The students followed as I walked the hall, pretending to be Jesus on the way to Jerusalem. We came back to the classroom, which was now the temple, one of the most amazing structures in the ancient world. But what was this? Loudly, "Jesus" proclaimed his anger and turned over

Turning tables in East Jerusalem—Marchers protest the demolition of
Palestinian homes by Israeli authorities. The girl's sign reads in Hebrew:
"There is nothing holy about an occupied city."

the Sunday school table! Everything went sliding to the floor and the children gathered uncertainly in the corner. An adult came running with a stern look on her face. "What's going on? Who's out of control? Do you need another adult?"

Jesus knew the temple should be a place for everyone to pray. I believe he was angry because the moneychangers were overcharging people with few resources, making it too expensive for them to pray to God (offer a sacrifice). I don't think Jesus' anger was primarily about selling things, but about the prices put on changing money and the offerings, on putting God beyond the reach of poor people. That is what made Jesus really angry. Greed and poverty were probably Jesus' most common topics and they were being played out at his father's house!

The students and I wondered awhile. Do people who don't have fancy clothes feel comfortable in our church? What if they smell bad or don't have money to put in the offering? If I were teaching this passage to adults I'd wonder what barriers we put in the way of people who want to take part in church activities. Might one be when our Sunday school class eats in a restaurant or has a retreat at a hotel? Is it our dress code or car code? Is it what we talk about after vacations?

Church grounds should not become a mall, but I'm not sure God is angry when our parking lot is used for a garage sale to support missions or when we purchase Fair Trade products on a Sunday morning. What Jesus was angry about was denying access to prayer and to God by putting financial barriers in the way.

The rest of the morning I sheepishly answered questions from people who heard the commotion. Bring the Bible alive and the church can barely handle it!

—*Susan Mark Landis*

Resurrection cookies

I used this recipe when my Sunday School class came to my house, although the children didn't stay overnight. We have not been able to track down the original author of this recipe, which is found in numerous places on the Internet.

- 1 cup whole pecans or almonds
- 1 teaspoon apple cider vinegar
- 3 egg whites
- pinch salt
- 1 cup organic sugar
- Plastic baggie
- Wooden spoon, rolling pin
- Tape
- Bible

Preheat oven to 300 ° F. (Do this before doing anything else.)
- Place nuts in baggie and beat them with a wooden spoon to break into small pieces. Explain that after Jesus was arrested, he was beaten by the Roman soldiers. Wonder what it feels like to beat someone and what it feels like to be beaten.
  Read John 19:1-3.
- Open the vinegar and let everyone smell it (or taste it, if they are brave!). Put 1 teaspoon into the mixing bowl. Explain that when Jesus was thirsty on the cross, all he was given to drink was vinegar.
  Read John 19:28-30.
- Add egg whites to the vinegar. Eggs represent life. Explain that Jesus gave his life to give us life.
  Read John 10:10-11.
- Sprinkle a little salt into each person's hand. Let them taste it, then brush the rest into the bowl. Explain that this represents the salty tears shed by Jesus' followers.
  Read Luke 23:27.
- So far the ingredients are not very appetizing. Sprinkle a little sugar into each person's hand. Let them taste it, then brush the rest into the bowl. Explain that the sweetest part of the story is that Jesus died

because he loves us and wants to show us how to live in love. *Read Psalm 34:8 and John 3:16.*

- Beat the egg white mixture with an electric mixer on high speed for 15 minutes until stiff peaks are formed. Explain that the tomb in which Jesus was laid was likely of white colored stone.

- Fold in nuts. Drop by teaspoons onto cookie sheets lined with parchment paper. Explain that each mound represents the rocky tomb where Jesus' body was laid.
Read Matthew 27:57-60.

- Put the cookie sheet in the oven; close the door and TURN THE OVEN OFF. Give each child a piece of tape and seal the oven door shut. Explain that Jesus' tomb was sealed.
Read Matthew 27:65-66.

- You're done! Explain that you cannot eat the cookies tonight, but that you have to leave the cookies in the oven overnight. That might not make anyone too happy. Explain that Jesus' followers were in despair when the tomb was sealed.
Read John 16:20 and 22.

- The next morning, open the oven and give everyone a cookie. Notice the cracked surface and take a bite. The cookies are hollow! On the third day, Jesus' followers were amazed to find the tomb open and empty.
Read Matthew 28:1-9.

- Enjoy the cookies! Ask the children to recount the story and how they felt as they waited to taste a cookie.

courtesy realfoodliving.com

Holy Week

Wednesday

Indian Springs, Nevada

Holy Week Vigil at Creech Air Force Base - 2009

At Creech Air Force Base in Nevada, forty miles northwest of Las Vegas, the Reaper (technically referred to as the "MQ-9 Reaper Hunter/Killer UAV") began practice runs at 7:06 a.m., taking off, circling, and landing every eighteen minutes throughout the morning. I had joined a group here to vigil and pray under the banner, "Ground the Drones."

Unlike the first Predator, an earlier unmanned aerial vehicle armed with two Hellfire missiles, the Reaper is capable of carrying fourteen Hellfire missiles. Flight crews of two, including a pilot and a technical support person called a sensor, sit here in rooms with several monitors and digitally guide these crafts as they move through their missions thousands of miles away in Afghanistan, Pakistan, and Iraq. During our vigil, U.S. Secretary of Defense Robert Gates announced a 127 percent increase in funding for drones and other digitally guided military hardware.

Our group enjoyed almost a cordial welcome from base workers, pilots, officers, and enlisted people as they entered and departed the base, but one man shouted at me on Tuesday, "Do you have any idea how many American soldiers' lives are saved every day by these aircraft?" I told him I didn't, and he advised me that the true number of saved service lives was twenty to thirty per day. I have not been able to confirm these numbers from any scientific source but I did remind him that the drone aircraft create enormous hostility in Afghanistan, Pakistan, and Iraq that will take generations to overcome. He was not impressed.

In the coming years the full implications of the U.S. military transformation to digital warfare will become apparent. The outrage we now see in the countries where they are used and the signs of trauma now becoming visible among soldiers, designers, and victims will signal a new era of brokenness and anger.

About three hundred yards down the road from the main entrance to Creech there is a small building set aside for two-week training programs for military chaplains who are about to depart for duty in Afghanistan and Iraq. The military chaplain is one of the first to be contacted by soldiers who are disturbed and morally shaken by what they experience in combat. Every month, dozens seek a way out and often encounter enormous difficulty and little support even from chaplains, all of whom come from religious traditions that teach love and reverence for life.

Like the chaplains, all of us who claim faith must discern what our responses can be in this new age of digital warfare. We will be further enabled to do this when our religious support structures—churches, denominations, and institutions—also reach deep into the humanizing and peaceful resources of holy tradition. The desert here in Indian Springs, Nevada where native people once came for water to sustain life is waiting for the transformation inherent in our faith.

—Gene Stoltzfus

"Through these gates pass America's finest warriors"

NOTICE
BY ORDER OF BASE COMMANDER

ENTRY PROCEDURES

Courtesy Gene Stoltzfus

Gene's beans

Boil soybeans for four hours or bring to a boil and allow to soak
for 12 hours, then boil again for two hours.
Beans can be frozen or kept in refrigerator for a few days, but not
too long.
Sauté onions and garlic in a frying pan.
Add pepper, red or black, to taste.
Put two to four cups of boiled soybeans in the frying pan.

Add:
1/3 cup soy sauce
1 tablespoon lemon or vinegar
2-3 tablespoons of honey, molasses, or sugar

Bring to boil, allow to simmer for 1/2 hour.

Serve over steamed rice.

This recipe can be changed to include curry, less soy sauce,
or other spices according to taste.
You can use soybeans directly from the field, of course,
after cleaning.

Amy Terry Glass

Elbows are for giving

Children are not always willing to ask forgiveness if they feel wronged, or to offer forgiveness when irreparable damage has been done.

Our children felt strong boundaries that didn't allow the transgressor to get closer, ruling out most nonverbal, physical steps of reconciliation. Any action that might imply accepting more responsibility than they felt appropriate was just not going to happen.

We are all grateful for the ritual that they developed when they were pre-schoolers—the elbow shake. They were willing to respond to another's request to "shake elbows" or to extend their own elbows.

Try it after an irritating interaction with a close friend or family member. Minimal physical contact is needed, but in the attempt to match and move elbows together there is an opening for smiles, for recognizing that we're all awkward sometimes, but it is in this dance of trying over and over that we are most likely to find joy, peace, and love.

—Deb Bergen

There is no sin in love

Then Joseph bought a linen cloth, and taking down the body,
wrapped it in the linen cloth,
laid it in a tomb that had been hewn out of the rock.
He then rolled a stone against the door of the tomb.

—Mark 15:46 (NRSV)

Holy Thursday should have been just like any other day. But for Marino, a Guatemalan worker in a restaurant in LaGrange, Ga., it was a day that changed the course of his life. Marino was a documented immigrant, drawn to America for wages far higher than he could earn at home. He came from a very poor, small village. He helped to support his wife and children and his mother. While Marino was working, he fell more than ten feet from a ladder and sustained severe head trauma.

Marino's brother Julio was also working in LaGrange, and I accompanied him to the intensive care unit. As we waited through the night, the medical staff at the hospital informed us that Marino's prognosis was not good. Marino was already brain dead, and his vegetative state was irreversible. Julio was in anguish. He needed to make a decision on behalf of Marino's young wife and four small children in Guatemala. Should he allow his brother to be taken off life-support systems? The words "What would Jesus do?" felt hollow. The walls of political borders separated him from the rest of his family, whose support he desperately needed.

Julio looked at me with tears of torment and asked what I thought he should do. Then he added the sobering statement, "Anton, I don't want to sin." I offered to help him locate a priest who could administer last rites to Marino as well as offer spiritual guidance for Julio's dilemma. It was late morning on Good Friday. Churches were preparing for holy services of the remembrance of the crucifixion of Jesus Christ.

When the priest arrived, Julio asked him what he should do about the difficult end-of-life decision. The priest's words were profoundly simple and pastorally comforting: "There is no sin in love." With that, and the assurance from the medical staff that Marino would feel no pain, Julio made the painstaking decision to entrust his brother to God and enable the body to take its natural course.

—Anton Flores-Maisonet

J. Daryl Byler

Gethsemane is a small garden outside the eastern wall
of Jerusalem at the foot of the Mount of Olives.
Gethsemane means "oil press" in Hebrew.
Jesus and his disciples often visited this grove of olive trees,
according to the New Testament.

Cynthia Freisen Coyle

Perhaps you feel weary and exhausted.
Receive God's **rest.**

Perhaps your life feels broken,
fragmented or riddled with conflict.
Receive God's **healing.**

Perhaps your life feels dry or dead.
Receive the water of **life**
that God offers in abundance.

—J. Daryl Byler

Water of life

Jesus got up from the table, took off his outer robe,
and tied a towel around himself.
Then he poured water into a basin and began to wash the disciples' feet and to wipe
them with the towel that was tied around him.
After he had washed their feet, had put on his robe, and had returned to the table,
he said to them, "Do you know what I have done to you?
You call me Teacher and Lord—and you are right, for that is what I am.
So if I, your Lord and Teacher, have washed your feet,
you also ought to wash one another's feet.
For I have set you an example,
that you also should do as I have done to you."

—John 13:4-5, 12-15 (NRSV)

The Bible often uses images of water as a source of rest, of healing, and of life itself (Acts 16, Revelation 22).

Water is the symbol that we often exclude from our communion table, but it was very much a part of the last supper that Jesus ate with his disciples. Before he shared the bread and wine, Jesus washed his disciples' feet.

Taken together, the symbols of bread, wine, and water offer us powerful images to sustain our Christian journey:

Rest–because our relationship with God is based on God's grace—not on our striving or deserving. We can also rest because we know that the ultimate outcome of our work depends on God, not on us. God is faithful to bring resurrection from the tragedies we encounter in our work.

Healing—because Jesus has broken down the walls that divide us from one another and has restored us to right relationship with God.

Life—itself because we are joined to the body of Christ and God's Spirit flows through us.

—*J. Daryl Byler*

Signs of brokenness

When Jesus saw his mother and the disciple whom he loved standing beside her,
he said to his mother, "Woman, here is your son."
Then he said to the disciple, "Here is your mother."
And from that hour the disciple took her into his own home.

—John 19:26-27 (NRSV)

I knew that when I visited Guatemala in May I would have to make a detour to meet Marino's grieving family. But as we approached the village of El Mamonal, I began to have doubts. How would the family receive this privileged stranger from a faraway land? What would I say? What would I do?

The first stop was to see Marino's mother. Before I could even formally introduce myself, she started crying loudly. The tears flowed from a pain no mother should experience. She showed me photos of Marino that she had hanging on the wall as a sort of shrine. Next to these pictures was the photo of her husband, who had also recently died. She showed me a picture of her two young sons in LaGrange, Ga., and talked about it as "the cursed land" because it had taken her sons away from her. She still lived in deep poverty, in spite of the help her sons had been offering with their income from the north. All I could do was hug, pray, and offer sincere condolences.

I went with her to the gravesite of Marino, a tombstone whose stone would not be rolled away. "*¿Porque? ¿Porque?*" Why? Why? was the only word Marino's mother would repeat through her anguished sobbing. Why, indeed, I thought. As darkness engulfed us and a Guatemalan rain shower began to fall upon us like tears from heaven, I, too, quietly asked the question that often has no reply.

Next, I visited Marino's wife and children. I expressed my own sorrow, as well as the sorrow of others that Marino had known. I had brought with me a small sum of money, collected from Marino's friends at the restaurant. I felt a tinge of guilt as I offered her the money.

I think my feelings of uneasiness came from the fact that as a global society, our economic system in North America still relies on cheap labor, often from poor countries. I believe that having to migrate to escape poverty or persecution is one more consequence of the Fall. The true tragedy of Marino's death is that he had to leave his wife and children in search of their daily bread, a search that should never have been necessary in the first place.

As I was leaving Marino's family, his mother pulled me aside into the street and asked me why she had not received any financial assistance. After all, she too was now a widower. I tried to explain to her how, at least in American culture, when a tragedy like this occurs we rarely think of the adult's parents, only the widow and orphans.

Another sign of brokenness.

—Anton Flores-Maisonet

Two of Islam and Judaism's holiest sites, Jerusalem's Dome of the Rock and the Western Wall, seen through barbed wire.

Counting the cost

Whoever does not carry the cross and follow me cannot be my disciple.
For which of you, intending to build a tower, does not first sit down and
estimate the cost, to see whether he has enough to complete it?

—Luke 14:27-28 (NRSV)

In these verses, Jesus, who well knew what his cross would cost him, cautions those of us who would be his disciples to "count the cost." In the words of Dietrich Bonhoeffer, what Jesus is talking about is "costly grace" as opposed to "cheap grace." In the opening of his classic book, *The Cost of Discipleship*, Bonhoeffer states, "Cheap grace is the deadly enemy of our Church. …The essence of grace, we suppose, is that the account has been paid in advance; and, because it has been paid, everything can be had for nothing. …Cheap grace is grace without discipleship, grace without the cross, grace without Jesus Christ…" (pages 45, 47).

There are costs involved in all aspects of life, and someone must pay these costs. For example, when I burn excess fossil fuel by driving a fuel-inefficient vehicle, driving more miles than I need to, or enjoying the freedom of driving alone rather than carpooling, there are costs. One cost is the increase in greenhouse gases in the atmosphere, resulting in climate change. Another cost is the increased demand for fuel, which raises prices for all, including the poor. Their costs for transportation and to heat their homes is increased as a result of my habit. Some of the cost of my lifestyle is being shifted to others.

Another example is that, while I can afford to pay a higher price for necessities such as food and clothing, if I insist on getting "always the low price, always" as is the slogan of a popular big box store, there is a cost. There is a cost in God's economy for a cup of coffee or a pair of jeans. My cheap clothing may have been produced in sweatshop conditions in a developing country. Or as is the case with commodities such as coffee, tea, and chocolate, I may reap the benefits of low prices, while the farmer and workers are paid a price so low that they cannot afford to feed their families or pay for schooling for their children. Part of the cost of my clothing or cup of coffee is being borne by others instead of by me.

The apostle Paul exhorts us in Philippians 2:4, "Let each of you look not to your own interests, but to the interests of others." Counting the cost means that we must recognize ways in which we are shifting some of the real costs of our lifestyle decisions unjustly onto others and change the way we do things. If we do not do so, then our discipleship is one of "cheap grace."

Not paying the full cost of our lifestyle decisions also undermines peace. Biblical peace—shalom—involves the material well-being of all humans. By shifting some of the costs of our lifestyles onto others, we reduce their well-being. As we live lives of injustice, we break our peace with God, who is a God of justice and requires us to be people of justice. As we harm the environment, we break shalom with God's creation.

So how can we begin to be disciples who count the cost? We begin, as always, by asking God to show us the ways our lifestyles are unjustly shifting some costs onto others, probably others who can least afford to bear the cost. Then we can take action to change our lifestyles.

By living in ways that bear the full, true cost of our lifestyle decisions, we bring peace and justice to others and model Christ's sacrificial love epitomized by his death on the cross. Not a bad thing to do anytime, but particularly at Easter!

—Tom Beutel

Action steps

Research makes a difference

1. Choose one item in your house: something you eat or wear or play with. Perhaps with other members of your household, research where this article came from, who was involved in producing it, and who benefits from the profit. Consider if there are ways you can help people in this chain better benefit from their labor.

2. Consider one way you routinely use energy and how you might use less energy and enjoy the process more.

Women going to the tomb

Trembling even as we scurry,
Whispering our fears,
The darkness overwhelms us.
The pre-dawn shadows we know from years of beginning the day's work.
Today we shudder from darkness of betrayal and dashed dreams,
Of violence and soldiers, cursing and hate, pain and agony of spirit,
Of silence in response to beseeching prayers,
Of weeping alone at a distance while the men ran away.

    Darkness overpowers yet today: poverty and racism,
    Violence, hunger, militarism, hate,
    Running and hiding from injustice lest we also be tortured.
    We don't know him! We turn our eyes away. We dare not know him.

"Be not afraid."
"Peace, be still."
Echo empty with the tomb in sight.
Nothing changed after all.
The miracles were fleeting.
He had no power to right the wrong.
We have no words left for prayer.
Death reigns. Death reigns.

Then we are thrown to the ground
By power unleashed and light breaking forth.
The tomb is empty
For the living is not among the dead.
Still we tremble with questions and fears.
Who will believe women?
Who dares pray to the once dead alive?
Who will believe if they must then act?

—*Susan Mark Landis*

J. Daryl Byler

100

Death defeated, death destroyed

But on the first day of the week, at early dawn, they came to the tomb,
taking the spices that they had prepared.
They found the stone rolled away from the tomb, but when they went in,
they did not find the body. While they were perplexed about this,
suddenly two men in dazzling clothes stood beside them.
The women were terrified and bowed their faces to the ground,
but the men said to them, "Why do you look for the living among the dead?
He is not here, but has risen.
Remember how he told you, while he was still in Galilee,
that the Son of Man must be handed over to sinners,
and be crucified, and on the third day rise again."
Then they remembered his words, and returning from the tomb,
they told all this to the eleven and to all the rest.
Now it was Mary Magdalene, Joanna, Mary the mother of James,
and the other women with them who told this to the apostles.
But these words seemed to them an idle tale, and they did not believe them.
But Peter got up and ran to the tomb;
stooping and looking in, he saw the linen cloths by themselves;
then he went home, amazed at what had happened.

—Luke 24:1-12 (NRSV)

We live in the span of history between God's convincing defeat of the powers of death, and their full and final destruction. The resurrection offers compelling proof that the powers of death are no match for God's authority. Their weakness has been exposed, their ultimate threat disarmed.

But if death has been defeated, why were there so many violent killings around the world this week? Or why does the military occupation of Palestine continue? Or why is there so much poverty and suffering in the world?

While the powers of death have been defeated, they have not yet been destroyed. For a time they retain residual power and influence in this world. Indeed, many still cling to greed, domination, force, and the threat of death as the best tools for protecting self-interests.

Perhaps a sports analogy is appropriate. The powers of death are like a previously undefeated team that arrogantly tramples its opponents all season long. The team seems invincible. In the final game of the tournament, it dominates a seemingly much weaker team—what kind of game strategy is suffering and a cross?—and prepares to declare itself the champion. But in the last minutes of the game, the "weaker" team rallies and wins an extraordinary victory. While the arrogant team has been defeated, it will live to play more games next season, perhaps still dominating for a time. But its power has been diminished by the memory of its indisputable defeat in the championship game. Its invincibility has been eroded.

Today in the face of war, famine, dispossession, occupation, injustice, and all that feels unfair, we cry out to God to act quickly and decisively to destroy what remains of death's powers. But God waits patiently, offering every opportunity for the enemies of the cross—which sadly too often include the Christian church—to come to their senses and embrace the ways of God's kingdom.

And we must wait, too, but not passively. By our words and actions, we boldly announce God's Easter victory over death—light has triumphed over darkness, truth over falsehood, love over hate, nonviolence over violence and the way of service over the way of domination.

Even now we are to live into the vision that God promised through the prophet Isaiah: "I am about to create new heavens and a new earth" (Isaiah 65:17). In God's new order, distress, sickness, death, displacement, domination, and violence will no longer hold sway. They will be replaced by joy, good health, long life, secure dwellings, and right relationships (vv.19-25).

Like Moses, we may not live to see God's promise fulfilled in our lifetimes. But Easter gives us a bird's-eye view of the new heaven and earth that God is creating. Death has been defeated! Death will be destroyed!

—*J. Daryl and Cynthia Byler*

Cynthia Friesen Coyle

"…as we consider the change in the crowds from Palm Sunday's cheers of 'Hosanna!' to Good Friday's jeers of 'Crucify Him!' we realize that every person must make a choice of which crowd they wish to be a part of…"

—Jon Twitchell

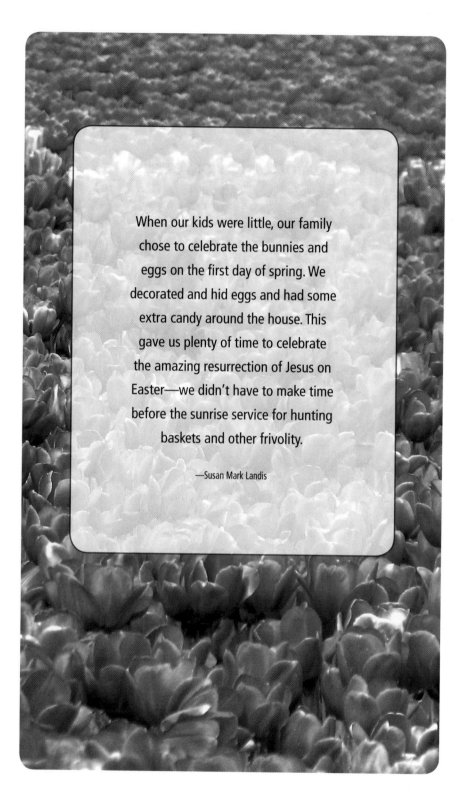

When our kids were little, our family chose to celebrate the bunnies and eggs on the first day of spring. We decorated and hid eggs and had some extra candy around the house. This gave us plenty of time to celebrate the amazing resurrection of Jesus on Easter—we didn't have to make time before the sunrise service for hunting baskets and other frivolity.

—Susan Mark Landis

He breathed on them

*When it was evening on that day, the first day of the week, and the doors of the house
where the disciples had met were locked for fear of the Jews,
Jesus came and stood among them and said, 'Peace be with you.'
After he said this, he showed them his hands and his side.
Then the disciples rejoiced when they saw the Lord. Jesus said to them again,
"Peace be with you. As the Father has sent me, so I send you."
When he had said this, he breathed on them and said to them,
"Receive the Holy Spirit.
If you forgive the sins of any, they are forgiven them;
if you retain the sins of any, they are retained."*

—John 20:19-23 (NRSV)

Alleluia! Christ is Risen!
With that great exclamation we begin each Eucharist throughout the entire season of Eastertide, which in the Anglican Communion (and in other churches) begins on Easter Sunday and lasts until the Sunday of Pentecost. That's a whole fifty days we get to celebrate Easter! I've always loved that Eastertide was longer than Lent. It just seemed right. So to all of you I wish a very blessed Eastertide.

The post-Resurrection stories in the four Gospels have always held a special place in my heart. They are filled with so much wisdom and love that after all these years of reading them, I still find so much in them to reflect upon, pray with, and, hopefully, base my life on.

One such story is that found in the Gospel of St. John. It is the evening of the first day of the week, the day we have come to call the first Easter, and the disciples are gathered together, hiding in fear for their lives. Back on Thursday night and Friday morning all but one had abandoned Jesus as he was arrested, tried before the Sanhedrin and Pontius Pilate, tortured, humiliated, made to bear his own instrument of death, crucified, and finally died. It is now Sunday night, their leader is gone, their own reputations destroyed, and each one of them must have been wondering, "Are they coming for me next?"

I have often wondered what it would have been like to have been hiding in that room with all those questions running through my mind. The apostles were so weak, so human, just like me. That's why I have always related to them. Each of them had committed themselves to following Jesus, and at the first sign of trouble, they fled from him. That, it seems to me, is a basic definition of sin: Not trusting in God when things get difficult. And so it seems totally appropriate to me that upon first entering through the locked door into that hiding place, the resurrected Jesus would address his disciples with a greeting of peace. With that simple "peace be with you" Jesus did so much for those very ordinary men: he forgave them. And in forgiving them he empowered them to be sent out to proclaim the Good News to all the world, just as the Father had sent Jesus to do the same. He empowered them to be workers for peace.

Then Jesus "breathes on them" and with this very intimate act, something he has done in other places when raising the dead or healing the sick, he communicates a kind of unity with all humanity. He tells his disciples that they are to "receive the Holy Spirit" by his breath. You see, we are united in the breath that is the Holy Spirit. This was more obvious to those who could read John's Gospel in the original Greek, for breath and spirit are the same word in that language. That breath is shared with all humanity.

Finally he instructs them, "If you forgive the sins of any, they are forgiven them; if you retain the sins of any, they are retained." In some circles within Christianity, that passage has been interpreted as one only applicable to those who are ordained. I have never read it that way. When I read this passage, I hear Jesus telling us one more time that we are united with one another, and with him in such a way that if we act to free our sisters and brothers from whatever it is that binds them to the sin and death and hell that they have brought upon themselves and others, then we are all free. If we insist on keeping our sisters and brothers chained to that same sin and death and hell, then they are chained, but so are we. If one is choking for lack of breath, we all suffocate.

So whether we are forgiving those who have harmed us, threatened us, or wished evil upon us; or if we are seeking forgiveness from those whom we have harmed, threatened, or wished evil upon, we are engaging in the creation of peace. We have the tools for peace within our reach. Jesus taught that to us in so many different ways, and the most basic tool he used was forgiveness. Whether we need to grant forgiveness or seek forgiveness from the neighbor who lives in our own home, down the street, or in another country, we have been given all we need to eventually live in a peaceful way. If we are to achieve peace before the sun goes down, we must first begin with forgiveness. This Eastertide, I invite you to allow Jesus to breathe on you and receive his greeting of peace. Then spread that breath around.

The Lord is risen indeed!

Alleluia!

—*Brother James Dowd*

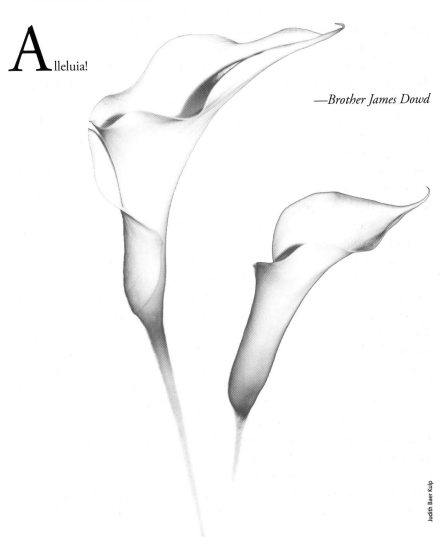

May

"Spring has returned.

The Earth is like a child

that knows poems…"

—Rainer Maria Rilke

Immigrant solidarity day

By the rivers of Babylon we sat and wept when we remembered Zion.

—Psalm 137:1 (NIV)

As I wrote this prayer, I reflected on my own journey as an immigrant in exile for 23 years. I also had in mind the book, *Devil's Highway,* by Luis Alberto Urrea, and his stories about the people crossing the desert and their journey to an unwelcoming land. Desolation is the word used in the book to describe the desert.

And I thought of my brothers and sisters at my church, who face these issues every day.

For the past few years, in the first week of May, we have celebrated Immigrant Solidarity Day. I offer this prayer to be used by other congregations during the first week of May, too.

As I pray this prayer, I am reminded of my own life experiences. I lived as a political refugee with my dad, mom, and four siblings in Mexico for three months in 1980, then as an immigrant in Canada from 1986 to 2001, and now as an immigrant in the United States since 2001.

My work with the MCC U.S. Office on Immigration Education allows me to walk hand-in-hand with fellow immigrants and others in exile in our struggle for restoration. Together we weep when we remember.

—*Saulo Padilla*

I walk with my brothers and sisters in desolation. Are you here, God?
Please don't be far. I am afraid and my soul is trembling.
You cried in Gethsemane, come cry with me.

Many hunt for us and we are accused of breaking the law;
You have been persecuted, come be our witness,
defend our cause.

Make known the roots of our suffering and the causes of our journey.
Make public that our intentions are in accord with your law.

Intercede for those who walk with us in this path.
Make their rights be known, and their voices be heard.

Guide the feet of those who get lost. You know the darkness.
Hold our hands. In the dim night shine your light and direct our path.

Restore the lands of our ancestors. Bring justice to our people.
Pour rain on their crops, and give them peace to harvest their fruit.

Anxiety and fear are our companions in our journey;
Replace them with peace and hope.

Nurture our spirits while we are far from home. Be with our loved ones.
Do not let time erase the way back home, so that we may not live in
exile forever.

The desert is arid and thirst awaits us. You know the desert.
You've been exiled. Come walk with us, and bring a fountain of justice
into our lives.

Sow seeds of peace and justice in the hearts and minds of those who resist
our journey. Let us be seeds of peace and hope in our new home, this land
of our exile.

Peaceful homes – a May Day card

Isaiah 32 creates an image of God's perfect plan for peace in our lives and homes—a beautiful image to share with others on May Day.

The fruit of that righteousness will be peace;
*   its effect will be quietness and confidence forever.*
My people will live in peaceful dwelling places,
*   in secure homes, in undisturbed places of rest.*

Here's a small note card you can make to share God's desire for us. Use it to send words of encouragement, as a thank you for a hostess, a house-warming or for a wedding.

To make the card:

Create a cardboard pattern for the basket patterns (one large triangle, two small triangles, and a half-circle handle).

Trace the pattern onto the back side of fabric scraps, decorative scrap book papers, wallpaper sample books, or construction paper.

Cut out the pieces. Use a glue stick to attach the basket pieces to the front of a blank note card.

Use a fine-point permanent ink marker to pen the Isaiah 32:18 scripture around the basket handle (as shown).

—Carol Honderich

Judith Baer Kulp

Perennials are just that—perennial. They are plants that keep popping up year after year. And they tend to spread. One year some gardeners in our church decided to have a backyard "perennial exchange." All were invited.

People with big, established gardens brought pots and boxes filled with pieces of perennial plants from their gardens for new gardeners. We exchanged plants, tips, and a potluck breakfast.

It was such a success that it became an annual event. Now when we go into each other's gardens, we often see plants that we recognize! We have purple irises from Mildred's garden, which often have wild poppies coming up in them. Jane's hostas are popular, as well as Helen's groundcover. I've forgotten the names of some of these plants, but I know where I got them. I can't remember who gave me those Chinese lanterns that are taking over the back corner of my garden! I wish I knew; I have some lovely mint to share with them!

—Carol Penner

Action steps

Recycle, be eco-smart, and stop hoeing!

1. Mix coffee grounds with leaves and grass clippings. (Get free coffee grounds at many coffee shops.)
2. Spread it on bare earth around perennials and between rows of vegetables to prevent unwanted weeds. Enrich the soil and hang up your hoe!
3. Don't rake out old roots and stems from last year. Mix them in, too.

Fish and eggs,
snakes and scorpions

"So I say to you, Ask, and it will be given to you; search, and you will find;
knock, and the door will be opened for you.
For everyone who asks receives, and everyone who searches finds,
and for everyone who knocks, the door will be opened.
Is there anyone among you who, if your child asks for a fish, will give a snake instead
of a fish? Or if the child asks for an egg, will give a scorpion?
If you then, who are evil, know how to give good gifts to your children, how much
more will the heavenly Father give the Holy Spirit to those who ask him!"

—Luke 11:9-13 (NRSV)

Much has been written about the Lord's Prayer, which precedes the above text, but little has been written about this part of Jesus' teaching using fish and eggs or snakes and scorpions as metaphor. Perhaps that is because the connection between the two is difficult to make and the comments in this text seem a bit far-fetched.

We know that tension exists between persistent prayers and the results from such strenuous effort. Sometimes there seems to be no correlation between praying and receiving our "fish" or our "egg." At the end of the text, up pops a promise that God will grant the Holy Spirit to those who ask.

What is going on? This is a devil of a text to understand.

Perhaps Jesus is saying that whatever the concrete specifics of our prayers may be, the crucial thing is that our hearts be aligned with God's heart and that we see our needs as the Holy Spirit sees them.

I believe Jesus is suggesting that our prayers are to be shaped by the Holy Spirit's influence and not by specific formulas or by external standards, even if the standards are set by holy people.

—*Richard "Dick" D. Davis*

Deviled eggs

Ingredients:
6 eggs
1/2 cup mayonnaise
1 1/2 teaspoons barbeque seasoning
1 tablespoon prepared Dijon-style mustard
2 tablespoons lemon juice
1 dash ground black pepper
1 (2.25 ounce) can sliced green olives, drained

Directions:
Boil 6 eggs. Cool and peel.

Slice eggs lengthwise. Remove yolks and place in a small bowl.
Using a spoon or fork, mash egg yolks.

Into the bowl with the egg yolks, mix mayonnaise, barbeque seasoning, prepared Dijon-style mustard, lemon juice, and ground black
pepper. Place the mixture in a plastic zipper bag. Cut one corner
from the bag, and squeeze the egg yolk mixture into the cooked
egg whites. Top with sliced green olives. Chill in the refrigerator
until serving.

—Richard "Dick" D. Davis

Judith Baer Kulp

Carol Penner

Savior in a swampy land

Jesus answered them, "Very truly, I tell you,
everyone who commits sin is a slave to sin.
The slave does not have a permanent place in the household;
the son has a place there forever.
So if the Son makes you free, you will be free indeed."

—John 8:34-36 (NRSV)

There's a swamp of secrets here stretching as far as the eye can see.
Secrets, crossed over with lies, half-submerged,
the muck of deception clings close
and there is something rotten in the state of grace.
You speak about your life, lightly,
and politely comment on the weather.
Your eyes tell a different story.
You are mired here, bone-mired,
in mud that will not let you go.
You are trapped and alone
and this may be the end.
>It's no good talking about the wise man who built on the rock.
>It's no good talking about the disciple who walked on the sea.
>It's no good talking about the tree planted by streams of living water.
What we need is a Jesus
like an amphibious tank
a thousand horsepower strong
roaring into view
spinning mud like geysers
clambering across every obstacle,
against all odds,
in this bleak landscape a vehicle of hope.

—*Carol Penner*

Peace with our own two hands

Turn from evil and do good;
seek peace and pursue it.
The eyes of the Lord are on the righteous,
and his ears are attentive to their cry;
but the face of the Lord is against those who do evil,
to blot out their name from the earth

Psalm 34:14-16 (NIV)

God of Wisdom,

As we remember the atomic blast, the gas chamber, the killing fields,

as we remember the war machine and the military establishment,

as we remember Hitler and Pol Pot, Jim Crow and the Indian Act,

call us to account for our own whispered innuendo,

our own snubs, our own finger pointing,

our own eyes averted from injustice, our own cutting words,

our own shove, our own furtive slap.

Do not allow the grandstand atrocities to blind us to our own cruelties.

From the darkness of our bedrooms to skyscraper boardrooms,

from schools and churches to houses of government,

give us ears to hear your call to peace in our time,

peace with our own two hands.

And now please join
me in the lighting

—*Carol Penner*

Bubbat

We got this recipe from Marlin Erin years ago. As I recall, they ate this on Sunday evenings in his Russian Mennonite tradition.

Ingredients
3/4 cup sugar
1 cup cream
1 cup milk
1 egg
3 1/4 cup flour
4 teaspoon baking powder
1 teaspoon salt
1 1/2 cup raisins

Directions
Mix sugar, cream, milk, and egg.
Mix flour, baking powder and salt separately and then add to milk mixture. Stir in raisins.
Bake in a 9 x 13" pan at 350 ° for 30-40 minutes.
This is especially good if eaten while still warm.

—Brenda Hostetler Meyer

Note: I couldn't wait and baked Bubbat this week. It's not quite scone, not quite coffeecake, and irresistible. For a lighter product, use all milk. If raisins are dry, moisten a bit first with boiling water. Dried cranberries or other fruit would add additional sparkle.

—Susan Mark Landis

May 5

The promise of abundance

I felt the heaviness of the room envelop me as I walked through the glass, double-doors, the security guard locking them behind me. It was 4 p.m. I was the last person allowed into the local Social Security office. The waiting room was still full; two long, silent rows; faces etched with anxiety, fear, and sadness; gloom wrapping them about like a shroud. This was recession personified.

Almost immediately, my name was called and I moved forward to claim the appointment I had made three weeks before. A woman, perhaps in her mid-50s, greeted me, then found my case on her computer. She turned to me expectantly. With anxiety tripping up my words, I began to describe why we couldn't possibly owe $36,000 of (allegedly) overpaid disability benefits from years before.

She listened carefully, jotted a few notes, then pulled up more data on her screen. I waited, trying to intuit what would come next.

I was astonished by what did come next. In the space of a few minutes and without an ounce of judgment, she replaced my anxiety with peace of mind. She understood why I was anxious, she said, but the next part of the process was hers to worry about. It was her job, in these next weeks, to figure out what happened and why; then she would work with me to decide how to address it. She promised to work with me until the end of the process. "It will be okay," she said simply. "You don't need to worry."

I stared at her, almost undone by her compassion. Feeling an immense sense of relief, I asked her, "How can you be like this, working with sad and difficult stories every day, all day long?"

Her eyes brightened and she leaned toward me as if sharing a secret. "I love my work," she said with passion. "At the end of every day I go home and know that I made a difference for at least one person that day. What could be better?"

I was deeply moved. The power of her spirit transformed mine. If the people in the outer room embodied the distress of the recession, the woman in this cubicle embodied the promise of abundance.

"Besides," she then added, with a grin, "They don't pay me nearly enough to be mean and grumpy."

—*Carolyn Schrock-Shenk*

A Maskil - of David

Happy are those whose transgression is forgiven,
whose sin is covered.
Happy are those to whom the Lord imputes no iniquity,
and in whose spirit there is no deceit.

While I kept silence, my body wasted away
through my groaning all day long.
For day and night your hand was heavy upon me;
my strength was dried up as by the heat of summer.
Selah

Then I acknowledged my sin to you,
and I did not hide my iniquity;
I said, 'I will confess my transgressions to the Lord,'
and you forgave the guilt of my sin.
Selah

Therefore let all who are faithful
offer prayer to you;
at a time of distress, the rush of mighty waters
shall not reach them.
You are a hiding place for me;
you preserve me from trouble;
you surround me with glad cries of deliverance.
Selah

I will instruct you and teach you the way you should go;
I will counsel you with my eye upon you.
Do not be like a horse or a mule, without understanding,
whose temper must be curbed with bit and bridle,
else it will not stay near you.

Many are the torments of the wicked,
but steadfast love surrounds those who trust in the Lord.
Be glad in the Lord and rejoice, O righteous,
and shout for joy, all you upright in heart.

—Psalm 32 (NRSV)

Peace and love

*Beloved, let us love one another, because love is from God;
everyone who loves is born of God and knows God.
Whoever does not love does not know God, for God is love.*

—I John 4:7-8 (NRSV)

If peace is God's ultimate end, surely love is God's ultimate means. For God, the end does justify the means; the only way to achieve true peace with justice is by love.

It should not surprise us that love is the most important Christian ideal. John 3:16 links the greatness of God's love for us to the gift of God's son, Jesus Christ. Of all the gifts, Paul says in I Corinthians 13:13, "the greatest of these is love." John says, "everyone who loves is born of God and knows God" and "God is love."

Jesus summed up the requirements of the law and the hope of the prophets as, "You shall love the Lord your God with all your heart, and with all your soul, and with all your mind" and "You shall love your neighbor as yourself" (Matthew 22:37-39).

To see love as the central ideal of our faith defines all that we do, including our peacemaking. When motivated by love, our peacemaking is done in ways that seek to provide what is needed and establish things as they ought to be. Peacemaking cannot be motivated by hatred, cannot exclude, cannot harm some to help others. Peacemaking in love seeks the prosperity of all, right relationships with all, well-being for all.

If peace is a state of things as they ought to be, and justice is providing what is needed rather than what is deserved, perhaps love is simply seeking the well-being of another. To love another is to say, "What can I do for you today that would provide for your well-being," and then to do it.

Love as a means of bringing peace goes well with Jesus' teachings that we should love our enemies. As we seek to understand the enemy and seek to act for his or her well-being, will that not promote peace?

And now peace, justice, and love abide, these three; and the greatest of these is love. Peace is our goal; justice is the measure of peace; love is our means of achieving peace.

—Tom Beutel

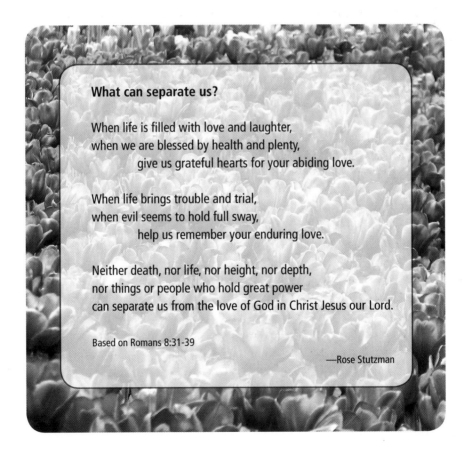

What can separate us?

When life is filled with love and laughter,
when we are blessed by health and plenty,
      give us grateful hearts for your abiding love.

When life brings trouble and trial,
when evil seems to hold full sway,
      help us remember your enduring love.

Neither death, nor life, nor height, nor depth,
nor things or people who hold great power
can separate us from the love of God in Christ Jesus our Lord.

Based on Romans 8:31-39

—Rose Stutzman

Love

If I speak in the tongues of mortals and of angels,
but do not have love, I am a noisy gong or a clanging cymbal.
And if I have prophetic powers, and understand all mysteries and all
knowledge, and if I have all faith, so as to remove mountains,
but do not have love, I am nothing.
If I give away all my possessions, and if I hand over my body so that I
may boast, but do not have love, I gain nothing.
Love is patient; love is kind;
love is not envious or boastful or arrogant or rude.
It does not insist on its own way; it is not irritable or resentful;
it does not rejoice in wrongdoing, but rejoices in the truth.
It bears all things, believes all things, hopes all things, endures all things.
Love never ends.
But as for prophecies, they will come to an end;
as for tongues, they will cease; as for knowledge, it will come to an end.
For we know only in part, and we prophesy only in part;
but when the complete comes, the partial will come to an end.
When I was a child, I spoke like a child,
I thought like a child, I reasoned like a child;
when I became an adult, I put an end to childish ways.
For now we see in a mirror, dimly, but then we will see face to face.
Now I know only in part; then I will know fully,
even as I have been fully known.
And now faith, hope, and love abide, these three;
and the greatest of these is love.

—I Corinthians 13 (NRSV)

We had regular, daily customers at work. Some were a pleasure to see. Others made all the employees scatter and hide. Whenever I felt that sinking dread at the sight of one of them, I tried to let that feeling serve as a reminder to have compassion and to pray for these people who were making my life so difficult.

—Audrey Hindes DiPalma

124

Open the gates of the kingdom

For the kingdom of God is not food and drink
but righteousness and peace and joy in the Holy Spirit.

—Romans 14:17 (NRSV)

I headed down the auto route from Strasbourg, France to Taizé, an ecumenical Christian community founded by Brother Roger 70 years ago. Today the community includes 100 brothers of both Protestant and Catholic traditions from more than 30 countries.

Over 100,000 youth make a pilgrimage here each year for worship, Bible study, and communal work. The Taizé songs are well-known among Christians around the world. I am attracted to the Taizé music because of its deep, spiritual longing for God's justice and peace.

During the weekend I was at Taizé, there may have been 500 youth there. In the summer, that number can grow to more than 5,000. Most live for a week in permanent tents. Basic food service relies heavily on volunteers for preparing and serving it. One morning I helped serve the breakfast of a bowl of cocoa, a baguette, and a small stick of chocolate.

While the food may be basic, the real entrée here is the three-times-daily worship, a liturgy that easily moved from French to German to English to Russian and back again. Repeated references to justice and peace and God's kingdom were interwoven with praise for God and joy in the Holy Spirit.

"I will walk in the presence of God and praise God in the land of life," we read from Psalm 116 in French and English, but with words printed for all to read in Italian, German, Spanish, Russian, Polish, and Latvian. "For the Lord is compassionate and good, our God is just and God defends the poor," we heard.

I learned that the ministry of the Taizé community extends well beyond its borders in southern France. It has a half-dozen outposts where brothers serve the poor in Bangladesh, the Philippines, Brazil, and elsewhere.

In another setting I heard pastor Natalie Francisco of Calvary Community Church in Hampton, Virginia, teach from I Chronicles 12 about the tribe of Issachar "who knew the times and knew what to do." These are times, I think, when Christians need to be clear about linking "joy in the Holy Spirit" and "God's kingdom of justice and peace." The Taizé community models this ability to link well.

Theology student Susan Kennel Harrison recently told me that my community, Mennonites, is diaconal in the world before they are theological. "We go do stuff and then we think about it later," she said.

Perhaps all Christians would be blessed if we were more intentional about holding together our joy and our work.

At Taizé, as the Eucharist was shared on Sunday morning, I knelt in front of the cross and thanked God for these brothers' ministry to youth and for their commitment to worship and service, for their intertwining of giving praise and seeking justice.

In closing we sang from our hearts, "*Beati voi poveri, perché vostro è il regno di Dio,* How blessed the poor in heart, for theirs is the kingdom."

For a brief moment, as the voices of God's people were raised in praise surrounding me, I could see how God had indeed opened the gates of the kingdom.

—Ron Byler

Ron Byler

"*Beati voi poveri,*
perché vostro è il regno di Dio."

"How blessed the poor in heart,
for theirs is the kingdom."

God of all nations

"Blessed be the Lord God of Israel,
for he has looked favorably on his people and redeemed them.
By the tender mercy of our God,
the dawn from on high will break upon us,
to give light to those who sit in darkness and in the shadow of death,
to guide our feet into the way of peace."

—Luke 1:68, 78 (NRSV), from the Canticle of Zechariah

Blessed are you, God of Israel,
for you have visited and redeemed your people

Blessed are you in planets that rise as bright as moons
Blessed are you in the gold that is the trees' first green
Blessed are you in the path of the south wind in new wheat
Blessed are you in one hundred shades of purple found in one bed of iris

Blessed are you, God of Gaza, of Hebron, of Ramallah and Jerusalem
Blessed are you, God of Fallujah, of Najaf, of Baghdad and Karbala

Blessed are you in shadows that shoot from stone walls of buildings
    almost as old as time
Blessed are you in olive groves and grape arbors and piles of oranges
Blessed are you in the drumming of oceans
Blessed are you in the endless shifting sculpture of desert sands

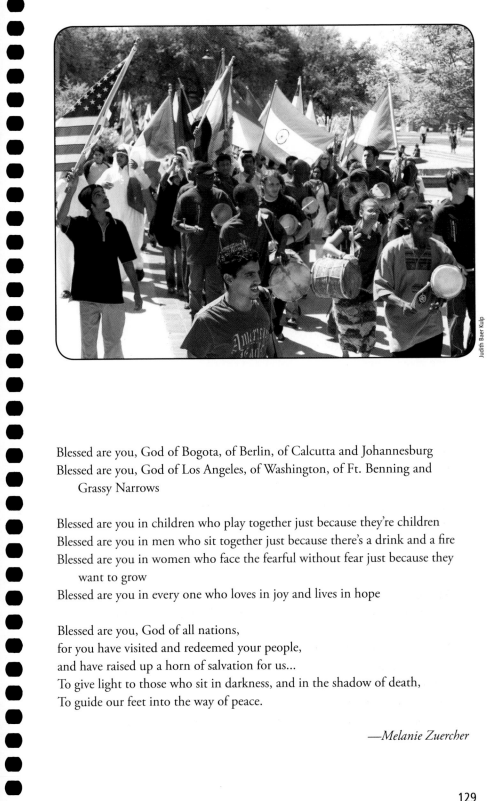

Judith Baer Kulp

Blessed are you, God of Bogota, of Berlin, of Calcutta and Johannesburg
Blessed are you, God of Los Angeles, of Washington, of Ft. Benning and
    Grassy Narrows

Blessed are you in children who play together just because they're children
Blessed are you in men who sit together just because there's a drink and a fire
Blessed are you in women who face the fearful without fear just because they
    want to grow
Blessed are you in every one who loves in joy and lives in hope

Blessed are you, God of all nations,
for you have visited and redeemed your people,
and have raised up a horn of salvation for us...
To give light to those who sit in darkness, and in the shadow of death,
To guide our feet into the way of peace.

—Melanie Zuercher

129

Mother's Day proclamation

Arise then...women of this day! Arise, all women who have hearts!
Whether your baptism be of water or of tears!

Say firmly:
"We will not have questions answered by irrelevant agencies,
our husbands will not come to us, reeking with carnage,
for caresses and applause.
Our sons shall not be taken from us to unlearn
all that we have been able to teach them of charity, mercy, and patience.

We women of one country will be too tender of those
of another country to allow our sons to be trained to injure theirs."

From the bosom of a devastated Earth a voice goes up with our own.
It says: "Disarm! Disarm!
The sword of murder is not the balance of justice."
Blood does not wipe out dishonor nor violence indicate possession.
As men have often forsaken the plough and the anvil
at the summons of war,
Let women now leave all that may be left of home
for a great and earnest day of counsel.

Let them meet first, as women, to bewail and commemorate the dead.
Let them solemnly take counsel with each other as to the means
whereby the great human family can live in peace.
Each bearing after his own time the sacred impress,
not of Caesar, but of God.

In the name of womanhood and humanity, I earnestly ask
that a general congress of women without limit of nationality,
may be appointed and held at someplace deemed most convenient
and the earliest period consistent with its objects,
to promote the alliance of the different nationalities,
the amicable settlement of international questions,
the great and general interests of peace.

—Julia Ward Howe, 1870

Sarah Witter

Action step

Honor a female peacemaker by writing her a note near Mother's Day, thanking her for nurturing you.

May 9

Piecing for peace:

A knitted log cabin prayer meditation

…pray without ceasing.

—1 Thessalonians 5:17 (NSRV)

When I was in high school, a sixth-grade boy named Luke taught me how to knit. From the beginning, I found knitting to be a soothing, meditative exercise. As I knit a project or a gift, I become increasingly calm and centered. I believe that when done intentionally and prayerfully, the act of knitting can also bring peace and wholeness to others and to the world around us.

The Knitted Log Cabin project is in the spirit of "Gathering up the Fragments" from the *More-With-Less Cookbook*, using leftover yarn from other projects, and can be used for anything from dishcloths and potholders, to afghans, lap blankets, or even scarves. I love the beauty of pieced quilts, so when I first saw a knitted log cabin square on Purl Bee's website, I fell in love. You can see it at: http://www.purlbee.com/log-cabin-washcloths/.

The technical aspects of this project are not that important. What is important is your intention and attention.

When sitting down to knit, you must first intend it as a time of prayer. Take a moment to say a prayer of dedication for this time. Secondly, keep your attention on what you're doing. You don't always have to be *saying* something to God, just holding the prayer in your heart as you pay very close attention to your stitching.

When other thoughts come up (and they surely will), gently, and without judgment, return your attention to your knitting and your prayer. In this way, you can pray without ceasing.

—*Audrey Hindes DiPalma*

Let's get started

Start by knitting a small square. Try to make it equal on all sides, as this will be the foundation for the whole log cabin block. Using all the same weight of yarn will help the finished block remain even, and allow for easier piecing with other finished blocks. Bind off the square except for the last stitch. Cut the yarn leaving a 4-6" tail. I know real knitters never tie knots. So if you are a real knitter, do whatever it is you do when changing colors. The rest of us can tie a new color to the old color with a knot.

With the new color, pick up stitches along the side of the square and knit rows until desired thickness. Keep track of how many rows this is so that all your 'logs' are the same. You'll soon get the feel for it and won't need to count anymore. No matter how thick your 'logs' are, after picking up the stitches, knit an odd number of rows, then bind off.

Again, leave one stitch at the end of the row that you are binding off, snip the yarn, attach a new color, and begin picking up stitches with the new color along the bottom edge of your original square. Continue knitting straight across the ends of 'logs', knitting your block as large or small as you like. When you finish, count up the 'logs,' starting in the center, to be sure you have the same number on each side. I weave in the ends on the back as I finish each block so that it is not an overwhelming task at the end.

Let's take it further

- You might have a list of people and/or situations to pray for when you sit down to knit. Dedicate one color or 'log' of the cabin to each. If doing a group project, come up with a list together.

- If making a gift for someone, keep track of the colors and tell them how you prayed for them with each one.
- If donating the project to an organization, focus your prayers and meditations on the work of that group.
- Engaging in any act in an attitude of prayer grounds us in the immediacy of God's presence. Knitting in particular is an activity whereby a long, wound-up ball of yarn is slowly transformed into something whole and beautiful, bringing peace to the world one stitch at a time.
- A tutorial and more detailed instructions can be found on my blog: http://wherethinplacesare.wordpress.com.

—Audrey Hindes DiPalma

Good guys or bad guys? It ain't that simple.

"Do not judge, so that you may not be judged.
For with the judgment you make, you will be judged,
and the measure you give will be the measure you get.
Why do you see the speck in your neighbor's eye,
but do not notice the log in your own eye? Or how can you say to your neighbor,
'Let me take the speck out of your eye,' while the log is in your own eye?
You hypocrite, first take the log out of your own eye,
and then you will see clearly to take the speck out of your neighbor's eye."

—Matthew 7:1-5 (NRSV)

The Toronto-based Globe and Mail ran a series on the future of Canada's military forces after they withdraw from Afghanistan. It raised the question, "Should our military kill bad people, or help the good ones?"

The question reminded me of the famous quotation of General Rick Hillier, that the job of the Canadian Forces (CF) in Afghanistan is to kill bad people, especially the "detestable murderers and scumbags."

We are the good guys; they are the bad guys.

I know that the Globe and Mail is trying to sell newspapers, but surely we know that the world is a whole lot more complex and that who is "good" and "bad" depends very much on one's perspective and worldview.

One of the things that invariably happens in war is the dehumanization of "the other." Soldiers need to overcome their aversion to killing others. The public needs to be willing to send its sons and daughters into harm's way. This is accomplished through vilifying and dehumanizing the enemy, and portraying our fight with that enemy as a battle of good against evil. We have witnessed a lot of this in the nine years that Canada has been fighting a war in Afghanistan.

I do not wish to defend the Taliban insurgents. I know that they are guilty of violating human rights and committing terrible crimes. I am horrified by the heinous acts they've committed against women and girls and the suicide attacks they've carried out against innocent civilians.

However, it is important to remember that the Taliban is not a homogenous group, and that many of its members are not the hard-core extremists we've been told they are. Many of the people who join the insurgency do so because of economic need. Afghan partners have told Mennonite Central Committee officials that this number could approach 90 percent. Others join because they resent political marginalization, they are disillusioned with the Karzai government, or because the promised aid from the West has not improved their lives in significant ways. They have legitimate grievances.

The point is that the Canadian government, military, and the media have served to demonize the Taliban and to portray it as the epitome of evil. They need to do that in order for continued support for an increasingly unpopular war.

A further point is that the international community and its military forces are not necessarily the good guys in all this. Sure, Canadian Forces have, for the most part, tried to operate according to the laws of war. But we know that the CF and the international coalition of which it is a part are not necessarily perceived by Afghans as the "saviors" that we want to believe they are, helping to rebuild a shattered country into a modern, prosperous, and democratic one.

A recent study by Open Society revealed that there is a growing "trust deficit" in Afghanistan. Afghans surveyed by researchers in six provinces in late 2009 and 2010 do not identify international forces as the "good guys," but increasingly regard them as the "bad guys." Their growing resentment results from what they know about the international forces' responsibility for civilian casualties, night raids, arbitrary detention, and the impunity that international forces seem to have.

The truth is that life—and war—is not about good guys and bad guys. Sure, there are some conflicts where one group may demonstrate a higher respect for life and the rule of law. But we do well to try to genuinely understand the other side and to also understand how the other side might perceive us. We will likely learn that the others are not all bad and that we are not all good. Hopefully, we will also learn that killing one another solves nothing and only leads to more killing.

Russian dissident and novelist, poet, and Nobel Peace Prize winner Alexander Solzhenitsyn said, "The line separating good and evil passes not through states, nor between classes, nor between political parties either, but right through every human heart, and through all human hearts." Perhaps as Canadians reflect on our participation in the Afghanistan War, we can set aside simplistic talk about good guys and bad guys. Let us learn to see ourselves as others see us, and let us learn to see the humanity in those whose views and actions we oppose. As long as Canadians continue to regard the world as divided between good guys and bad guys, we will not contribute much toward global peace.

—Esther Epp-Tiessen

MCC photo - Sarah Adams

Children line up for lunch at Le Pelican — Based in Kabul, this Mennonite Central Committee partner provides education for mostly Hazara (a marginalized group in Afghanistan) children who would not otherwise attend school. This includes children with disabilities as well as children whose academic level does not meet their age and who are therefore not able to attend normal government schools. In addition to general subjects taught, Le Pelican offers the children a healthy lunch each day, recreation, special classes on topics like hygiene, parties, skills training (in the form of a successful bakery), and medical support through a small on-site pharmacy.

God's plea

"As a mother comforts her child,
so I will comfort you;
you shall be comforted in Jerusalem."

—Isaiah 66:13 (NRSV)

God calls to us and says:

As a mother comforts her child,
so I long to comfort you,
I long to comfort you at home.

Don't you remember?
I taught you to walk,
I took you up in my arms and healed you.
I led you with cords of human kindness, with bands of love.
I was like those women who lift babies to their cheeks.
I bent down to you and fed you.

If only you would return to me.
Like a hen, I would gather you under my wings.
I would give you shelter and peace.

Based on Isaiah 66:13, Hosea 11:3-4, and Luke 13:34

—*Linda Gehman Peachey*

Thai fried noodles

Bring 6 cups of water to boil in a large pot. Add 8-10 ounces flat rice noodles (the width of spaghetti) and cook for 3-5 minutes until soft but not mushy. Drain and rinse with cold water. Let stand at room temperature until needed.

Prepare ahead, so they are ready to add at the end:
2 ounces bean sprouts
3 tablespoons chopped green onions
2-3 tablespoons chopped cilantro
3 tablespoons chopped roasted peanuts.
Set aside until ready to serve.

In wok or large frying pan:
Heat 2 tablespoons oil.
Add 2 cloves minced garlic.
Add 1/4 -1/2 pound sliced chicken breast or pork and fry until cooked through.
Add 1 cup sliced carrots and 1 cup green or red pepper.
Fry about 3 minutes.
Reduce heat.

Mix together:
3 tablespoons lemon juice
5-6 tablespoons Asian fish sauce (available in many larger grocery stories and Asian markets)
2 tablespoons sugar
Add to meat and vegetables, stir gently until heated through and the vegetables are crisp-tender.
Add the drained noodles and heat through.

If desired, beat 1-2 eggs, fry very thin and slice in long strips to place over the dish. Sprinkle the green onions, cilantro, and peanuts over everything. Garnish with cilantro and lime wedges and serve immediately.

—Linda Gehman Peachey

The message of peace

is far too serious to be left to anyone

but clowns, artists, and mystics.

Travel in their company.

—Mary Lou Kownacki, OSB

Tim Nafziger

A broad place

Out of my distress I called on the Lord;
the Lord answered me and set me in a broad place.
With the Lord on my side I do not fear. What can mortals do to me?
The Lord is on my side to help me;
I shall look in triumph on those who hate me.
It is better to take refuge in the Lord than to put confidence in mortals.
It is better to take refuge in the Lord than to put confidence in princes.

—Psalm 118:5-9 (NRSV)

When our checking account balance gets low or my schedule gets packed or my options feel limited, I often become anxious, fearful, angry, and less gracious in my relationships.

Will we have enough money to make it to the next pay period?
Will I have enough time to get everything done?
Will I have any meaningful choices?

Scarcity creates tension. Indeed, scarcity is the root of much global conflict.
Scarcity of natural resources–land, water, and oil–spawns many wars.
Scarcity of jobs, as in the current U.S. economy, often results in hostile
    treatment toward recent immigrants.
Scarcity of hope leads some to resort to violence in the hope of having their
    voices heard.
Scarcity of justice or respect for human rights has led to popular uprisings
    in many countries.

Government policies can contribute to our sense either of scarcity or of enough for all. High levels of military spending, for example, strip funds away from programs that would offer educational or housing opportunities. John Perkins, founder of Voice of Calvary Ministries, has reminded the church for many years that poverty is, at its core, the scarcity of opportunities. Consistent support for civil and human rights, on the other hand, creates the space for people to flourish.

The Psalmist wrote frequently about scarcity. Many psalms reflect the feeling of being trapped; the looming sense that enemies are closing in, that space is tight, resources are limited, or options are shutting down. In the midst of scarcity, the Psalmist declares that God is the one who offers space—a broad place.

"Answer me when I call, O God of my right! You gave me room when I was in distress," declares David (Psalm 4:1). "And you have not delivered me into the hand of the enemy; you have set my feet in a broad place," he continues (31:8). "Out of my distress I called on the Lord; the Lord answered me and set me in a broad place," the Psalmist confesses (118:5).

In the face of scarcity:
> God offers generous provision for our needs (Psalm 103:3-5).
> God offers justice for the oppressed (Psalm 140:12).
> God offers deliverance from our enemies (Psalm 33:16-20).
> God offers hope for the despairing (Psalm 42:5, 11).

God has created the world with enough for all its inhabitants. It is human greed and injustice that lead to scarcity. As Christians, we join with God in offering one another a broad place—
> When we share generously of our resources,
> When we act justly with whatever power has been entrusted to us,
> When we use our gifts to create opportunities for those with limited options,
> When we offer God's hope to those who are downcast.

Doing these things is the basis for our appeal to governing authorities. Doing these things gives integrity to our appeal for public policies that create a sense of enough rather than contributing to the sense of scarcity.

By our lifestyles, actions and advocacy, will we contribute to the scarcity which spawns conflict? Or will we choose, along with God, to offer a broad place for our sisters and brothers around the world?

—*J. Daryl Byler*

Survivor for peacemakers

The Lord God has sworn by himself
(says the Lord, the God of hosts):
"I abhor the pride of Jacob
and hate his strongholds;
and I will deliver up the city and all that is in it."

—Amos 6:8 (NRSV)

I have a confession. Lately I've been watching *Survivor*, that popular television reality show. Normally, I am not a connoisseur of crass TV (okay, I've seen a few episodes of *The Apprentice* too), but in the midst of trying to figure out what all the fuss is about I stumbled upon larger meaning.

Survivor is a game whose players are stranded on a remote island and divided into two tribes. With few resources, each tribe must cooperate in scavenging for food, building a shelter, and competing against the other tribe. If, however, their tribe loses a "challenge," they must vote one of their tribe-mates out of the game. The last survivor wins.

Each episode I've seen is filled with unsettling mixtures of trust and betrayal, sacrifice and self-preservation as contestants decide how to play the game. Alliances are made and broken, and before long, all contestants are watching their backs. But here's the lesson *Survivor* taught me: success breeds conceit, and conceit will be your downfall. Invariably, players gain power and think they control their destiny, only to be abruptly voted off by their tribe. Few sins are less forgivable, it turns out, than arrogance.

As I ponder this over my morning newspaper, larger questions emerge. How is the country of my birth, the world's superpower, like the brash *Survivor* contestant? Are we a little too sure of our power? Have we claimed for ourselves the ability to control not only our destiny but the destinies of other countries as well? And if so, what's a U.S.-American Christian to do?

One needn't discount all that is admirable about the United States—its ideals, its freedoms, its image of hope and opportunity for many in the world—to acknowledge its incessant propensity toward arrogance. Our leaders rarely apologize, repent, or acknowledge malfeasance. Both Democrats and Republicans regularly intervene in foreign countries in ways we would never tolerate if the tables were turned. And in the last decade, the United States has affirmed unilateral, preemptive warfare as a legitimate foreign policy option. Arrogance of this sort can undermine even our best qualities.

Perhaps not surprisingly, a public opinion poll taken by the Pew Research Center for the People and the Press found that citizens of Europe and the Middle East are registering increasingly higher levels of antagonism toward the United States. In the world court of public opinion, "the tribe has spoken" and their word stands as a warning to the abuses of arrogance.

Stories of national arrogance are as old as the Bible. In one chapter it could be Assyria and in the next Israel, but the condemnation of God is consistent. "Thus says the Lord: I will ruin the pride of Judah and the great pride of Jerusalem. This evil people, who refuse to hear my words, and who stubbornly follow their own will…shall be like this loincloth, which is good for nothing" (Jeremiah 13:9-10).

I do not expect politicians to repudiate superpower arrogance. They have a game of *Survivor* to play, following a time-honored script of promise-making and mudslinging.

But followers of God are given a different script. The biblical response to pride is to humble oneself (Luke 18:14, James 4:6) and associate with the lowly (Romans 12:16). This has political as well as personal ramifications. It suggests that we are not deserving of a disproportionate share of the world's resources simply because we're Americans. And it calls us to stand with the poor, the marginalized, and the undocumented, offering compassion and advocacy. Micah puts it best: "What does the Lord require of you but to do justice, and to love kindness, and to walk humbly with your God?" (Micah 6:8).

As a follower of the way of the cross, we acknowledge that Jesus was a loser in the world's game of *Survivor.* But the glory of Easter is that God plays by a different set of rules.

Do we?

—*Karl S. Shelly*

Word become flesh

The Lord looks down from heaven; he sees all humankind.
From where he sits enthroned he watches
all the inhabitants of the earth—
he who fashions the hearts of them all, and observes all their deeds.
A king is not saved by his great army;
a warrior is not delivered by his great strength.
The war horse is a vain hope for victory, and by its great might it cannot save.

—Psalm 133 (NRSV)

I've been reading an anthology of selected writings of Thomas Merton. I came upon the following, from *New Seeds of Contemplation*, published in 1961, during some of the hottest days of the Cold War.

"…we build up such an obsession with evil, both in ourselves and in others, that we waste all our mental energy trying to account for this evil, to punish it, to exorcise it, or to get rid of it in any way we can. We drive ourselves mad with our preoccupation and in the end there is no outlet left but violence. We have to destroy something or someone. By that time we have created for ourselves a suitable enemy, a scapegoat in whom we have invested all the evil in the world. He is the cause of every wrong. He is the fomenter of all conflict. If he can only be destroyed, conflict will cease, evil will be done with, there will be no more war."

I read this as the news came out about the horrifying abuse of Iraqi prisoners by U.S. military personnel at the Abu Ghraib prison near Baghdad. On May 7, 2004 The Wichita Eagle published The New York Times photograph of Private Lynndie England holding a leash around the neck of a naked Iraqi prisoner lying on the ground. The page three Times headline about England, who is from Fort Ashby, W.Va., reads, "Town wonders how one of its own is part of Iraq scandal."

A friend of England's is quoted, "It's so not her. It's not in her nature to do something like this."

That friend is right. If we believe all human beings are created in the image of God, then it necessarily follows that it is in the nature of no one to be as cruel and vicious as Lynndie England appears in that photograph.

But along the way, she—and all of us, in some fashion—somehow learned to see other children of God as evil, less than human, and worthy of cruel treatment. We have driven "…ourselves mad with our preoccupation [with evil]" and "there is no outlet left but violence" and destruction.

This kind of violence is woven into the very fabric of U.S. society, and as such it comes out in every facet of that society, from the military to the marketplace to the media, in law enforcement, in school gyms, in church. It comes out as dehumanization, leading to the assumption that the individual cruelty of torture and the mass violence of war against those who are "less than human" is acceptable. It comes out in the arrogance that assumed viewers would approve of photos showing the torture of Iraqis, photos that were presumably taken to be displayed and designed to utterly humiliate the Muslim victims. It's indelible in popular culture; on TV and in movies, in video games and comic books, on billboards and in magazines. It goes far in explaining to Fort Ashby, W.Va., and to every town and city in this country, why some of its soldiers have behaved the way the evidence seems to show they have. Why should they not live out in their daily lives and actions what nearly every part of their culture has taught them is all right?

In *New Seeds of Contemplation,* when Merton wrote about "the suitable enemy," he was not applauding that perspective, but was mourning it. He gave us Western Christians our challenge when he wrote, in *Good Work,* "Since the Word was made flesh, God is in [humanity]. God is in all [humanity]. All [people] are to be seen and treated as Christ. Failure to do this, the Lord tells us, involves condemnation for disloyalty to the most fundamental of revealed truths."

We all—yes, all we Christians—are implicated in the culture that produced the abuses at Abu Ghraib. We have much to confess and much to repent. No, it isn't an easy challenge to take. But then, it never was.

—*Melanie Zuercher*

Cynthia Friesen Coyle

"At the root of all war is fear."

—Thomas Merton

And how shall I boast?

Let the believer who is lowly boast in being raised up,
and the rich in being brought low,
for the rich will disappear like a flower in the field.

—James 1:9-10 (NRSV)

I recently read this passage, and as often happens when I read the Bible, it jumped off the page at me. I pondered the meaning of these verses. Is James suggesting that redistributing wealth is something we should strive for? Or is this simply a way of reminding us of the temporal nature of life itself?

Life is fleeting in nature. No matter what we accumulate, we can't take any of it with us after our hearts stop beating. Yet, as we look at the context of the book of James, we must conclude that there is more here than a mere reminder that life is comparatively short. It is important for the lowly (the poor?) to be raised up, and equally important for the rich to be "brought low" since both the lowly and the rich are being asked to boast about this equalization.

Is this a concept we can embrace as peacemakers?

I find it very difficult for me to accept the reality of my wealth. When I compare myself to others with my same education and age, I have very little in the way of assets or income. But I find it more difficult to compare assets and income to those who have so much less than I do. In the United States, there are so many rich and super-rich people, it is easy to think we have relatively little. But for a moment, let's be honest: most of us, by world standards and by U.S. standards, are rich.

If we are rich, are we willing to boast about being "brought low"? Or is the idea of wealth redistribution for others, not for peacemakers? In Luke 14: 28-33, Jesus tells us to count the cost before we begin our journey with him.

Is James 1:9-10 a scripture we as peacemakers should consider as we count the cost of walking the path of peace and justice with Jesus?

—*Patricia Burdette*

Peacefulness

I have the pleasure of a canine assistant in my child psychiatry office. Her trainers were nervous about whether she'd pass the required tests, because she is strong-willed and a creative tease. Although she beheaded more than one of my plastic dinosaurs, when she had to take a couple of weeks off there were even more broken toys.

She centers children who are hyperactive or anxious. Children who have experienced adults as untrustworthy are more comfortable with her wordless interactions. Even the most hesitant adults are won over by her quiet warmth as she sleeps near their feet.

Her sensitivity to tension makes my office an unusually calm place within our family services building. At the first harsh phrase or raised voice, she lifts her head to look at the offender, and even the most agitated person calms down so the dog won't be disturbed. She reflects back the capacity to be gentler and the advantages of choosing to communicate differently. Her relaxation is all the immediate feedback patients need.

I'm not suggesting you rush out to get a pet. Peace is not nurtured when dogs bark at all hours in the neighborhood, cats aggressively expand territory, or families fight over animal chores. What we can do is increase the presence of nonhuman creation in our lives.

Research is clear that stopping to smell fragrant flowers increases peacefulness because of our deep breaths and focus. Green plants purify air and moderate temperatures indoors and out. Bringing seasonal changes into your inside space keeps you connected to the wider world.

Knowing these benefits, it's a good idea to find a way to cultivate and share plants. Try to connect with animals a little bit every day, and find ways to play or work with one at least once a week.

Jesus pointed us to how God cares for what we may consider inconsequential, not even recognizing it as something that might nurture someone who feels overwhelmed: consider the flowers of the field and the birds of the air.

—Deb Bergen

Sarah Witter

The wolf shall live with the lamb,
the leopard shall lie down with the kid,
the calf and the lion and the fatling together,
and a little child shall lead them.

—Isaiah 11:6 (NRSV)

May 16

Miracles

"You have heard that it was said,
'You shall love your neighbor and hate your enemy.'
But I say to you, Love your enemies and pray for those who persecute you
so that you may be children of your Father in heaven;
for he makes his sun rise on the evil and on the good,
and sends rain on the righteous and on the unrighteous."

—Matthew 5:43-48 (NRSV)

He's a Marine Corps veteran of eight years. He spent two and a half years in Iraq. He hates police, all Iraqis, and his alcoholic father who abused him during his childhood. Increasing his stress load are physical, employment, family, money, and housing problems.

He is a white person assigned to our anger management program because of his disruptive, degrading, racist remarks. He's in a class the court required him to take because of his fight-starting remarks to black, fellow prisoners.

To provide him an opposite view (of those who hate white people), we looked at videos of Native Americans and African Americans who were victims of terrible wrongs by whites like him. Their ability to replace hatred with empathy was hard for him to understand.

We have not condemned his racial prejudice; we have not been as intolerant of him as he is of others. And that may be the most helpful to him—not giving him what he expected from us. The challenge is to respect him when he shares his bigotry.

Without trying to change him, we simply respond that we can't share his views; we haven't been through what he has.

Now we are trying "I" statements: practicing saying how I feel without defending myself or trying to win arguments. "I feel Hitler was right about white superiority. That is just the way I feel." Or, "I'm sorry but I can't work with black people. I'm racist."

Of course, I also am racist in ways I don't recognize. He and I don't know yet if he can be honest about how he feels instead of being insulting and belligerent. Or if he can become vulnerable and calmly accept the responses he gets. We are looking for a way he can be open with others who are different.

I believe we are looking for Jesus' patience and healing, and know miracles might happen to both of us.

—Stan Bohn

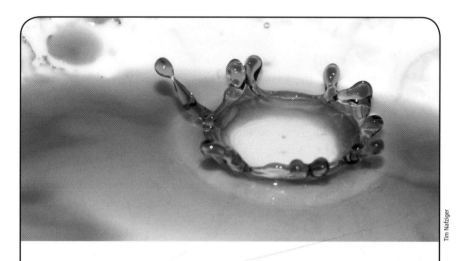

He drew a circle that shut me out.
Heretic, rebel, a thing to flout.
But Love and I had wit to win:
We drew a circle that took him in.

—Edwin Markham

May 17

Moral values

Good leaders abhor wrongdoing of all kinds;
sound leadership has a moral foundation.

—Proverbs 16:12 (The Message)

"In our religion, we also teach the importance of moral values, but we don't focus on only a few as though they were the truly important ones and the others are secondary. We, too, believe that abortion is a moral issue; but so are lying, war, over-consumption, exclusion, and unequal sharing of resources. These issues destroy the life of children just as surely as abortion does, and in our faith we take them very seriously."

This sharing from a Buddhist friend came after she observed a presidential campaign in the United States and was perplexed at the apparent focus on one or two moral values by U.S.-Americans in determining for whom to vote.

Her views are shared by many people here in Asia who believe that U.S.-Americans become deeply embroiled in one or two issues and then cannot step back and look at the big picture. During the presidential campaign, Asians watched with some incredulity as the loudest debates focused around two main issues: abortion and the definition of marriage. To people in Asia, these are also important moral issues, but they find it strange that the election of a nation's leader would hinge so much on just these two.

Isn't the death of thousands of women and children in Iraq since the 2003 U.S. invasion and subsequent occupation also a moral issue? they ask. According to researchers from Johns Hopkins Bloomberg School of Public Health in Baltimore, more than 100,000 people have died in Iraq due to military action since the invasion. A large number of the dead were women and children, the majority of them killed because of air strikes.

Should this moral issue not be given as much attention as abortion? Do not our scriptures teach us that what we do to the "least of these," we do to Christ?

There is also the very important moral issue of the use of our world's resources. We Americans consume an inordinate amount of the world's food supply.

Even though there is enough food being produced to ensure every human being an adequate amount, we Americans are overfed while millions go hungry. For example, the average U.S. citizen consumes more than three times the global average of 81 pounds of meat per person per year. Africans consume less than half the global average, and South Asians consume the least, at less than 13 pounds per person per year. These inequalities do not go unnoticed by the people of India, Bangladesh and other Asian countries. They see on their televisions the struggle of Americans trying to deal with obesity, while at the same time they live daily with people on the brink of starvation.

For them, this is a serious moral issue. They want to know: Why does food inequality not enter into the debates of the presidential candidates?

Perhaps we Christians feel more secure raising as moral issues those things with which we are personally most uncomfortable. While such moral issues are certainly important and call for serious attention, our focus on them should not distract from other moral issues which Christ raised so often and so powerfully, but which may tend to disturb our relatively comfortable lives.

How about a presidential debate reflecting on Christ's call to love our enemy, turn the other cheek, live with true humility or stand with the poor and oppressed? This would broaden the discussion about moral values to become more inclusive and more reflective of Christ's ministry on earth. Such discussions would also speak more powerfully to those of other faiths who want to know how the Christian faith responds to injustice of all kinds. It would also speak to answers of hope we, who profess a life in Christ, can bring to a very troubled and conflict-ridden world.

My answer to my Buddhist friend can only be this: Yes, we Christians too often do allow ourselves to argue about one or two important matters while ignoring others of equal or even greater significance. Perhaps we can be challenged by you in Asia to open our eyes to broader issues of moral values, so that our faith can become more complete and our witness to our threatened world more Christ-centered.

—Max Ediger

Letting go

Let the same mind be in you that was in Christ Jesus,
who, though he was in the form of God,
did not regard equality with God as something to be exploited,
but emptied himself, taking the form of a slave, being born in human likeness.
And being found in human form,
he humbled himself and became obedient
to the point of death—even death on a cross.

—Philippians 2:5-8 (NRSV)

Judith Baer Kulp

A prayer of release

How tightly we grip…whatever we can get our hands on, God.
Our need to accumulate, store up, pile on
never seems to be satisfied.
Over and over,
we think to ourselves, "Yes. I've finally got it,"
certain that success, or satisfaction, or happiness,
is now ours.
A moment passes, a day, a week,
and we find ourselves restless again,
searching again,
discontented again.
O God.
Thank you for the holy dis-ease
that prevents us from being content with what doesn't matter or last.

Listen to us under all our grabbing,
and turn your ear toward our deepest longings
even when we don't know them ourselves.
Answer our needy prayers
by loosening our grip and easing our grasping,
by growing in us the trust that you alone protect and provide.
In your great compassion, show us our place as a few among many
whether friends or enemies
so that we will know ourselves welcomed and beloved
along with all your other children
rather than at their expense.
We pray all this in the name of the One who showed us how to let go,
and through the power and companionship of your own Holy Spirit.

Amen.

—*Rachel Miller Jacobs*

Stone soup

Our desire is not that others might be relieved while you are hard pressed,
but that there might be equality.
At the present time your plenty will supply what they need,
so that in turn their plenty will supply what you need.
Then there will be equality.

—2 Corinthians 8:13-14 (NIV)

One of my favorite activities for young children is a Stone Soup party. I tell my own version of the "Stone Soup" folktale. It is a story about tired travelers in need of a meal who stop in a village where the crops have failed. There is so little food that everyone is hoarding and hiding what little they have. The travelers offer to make a magical soup that requires only a "soup stone" and water. As they keep tasting the soup, the travelers agree that it would taste even more wonderful if it had a bit of onions or beans. As villagers volunteer their meager resources, the soup becomes ever more delicious until by the end it's a feast.

As children arrive for the Stone Soup party, I immediately get them working on chopping vegetables into tiny pieces. As they work, I tell the story. After all the vegetables are chopped, we put them in plastic tubs and hide them around the room or the yard and get ready to act out the story. The soup pot is prepared with a scrubbed stone and boiling water.

As I tell the story, the children play the parts of the travelers or the villagers. They run to find the hidden vegetables and offer them into the community pot.

As we eat the delicious stone soup with homemade bread, we have time to talk peace. We talk about sharing what we have, so everyone has enough. We talk about community. We talk about how differences in flavors make the soup better.

In my own family, the scrubbed "soup stone" sits permanently on the back of the stovetop and is added to every vegetable soup. No one ever complains about eating vegetables if it's called Stone Soup.

—Jeanne Zimmerly Jantzi

Stone soup

ground beef or chicken (optional)
beef bouillon or broth or vegetable broth
any combination of:

	carrots	onions	peas
	celery	corn	potatoes
	cabbage	beans	tomatoes

Chop vegetables in tiny pieces so they will cook quickly. A hand-operated
food chopper makes it possible for even little ones to participate. For
very little children, provide already-boiled potatoes, which can be cut
easily with a plastic knife.
Add salt and pepper to taste.
Serve with homemade bread and fruit.

This is a good summertime, backyard, picnic table, campfire activity. If
the children are very small, it's better to do the acting away from the
real fire and put it all on the stove after you've mixed it up and acted
it out. This is a good activity for families to do together or for times
when you have groups of children in a range of ages.

—Jeanne Zimmerly Jantzi

Judith Baer Kulp

157

No longer afraid?

Finally, all of you should be of one mind.
Sympathize with each other. Love each other as brothers and sisters.
Be tenderhearted, and keep a humble attitude.
Don't repay evil for evil. Don't retaliate with insults when people insult you.
Instead, pay them back with a blessing.
That is what God has called you to do, and he will bless you for it.

—1 Peter 3:7-9 (New Living Translation)

As Kingman drove us along the road running from east to west across the island of Sri Lanka, he mused, "I find myself in a very bizarre situation. All of my activist life I have been anti-American policy, but now I find myself saying very positive things about the role of the U.S. military in our post-tsunami recovery."

Friends for more than 20 years, Kingman and I were meeting again after a long hiatus. Traveling to the east coast to visit tsunami-affected villages, I had opportunity to hear him reflect on his years of experience struggling on behalf of the oppressed Tamils in Sri Lanka. I asked him to elaborate on why he and so many others in Sri Lanka had developed such negative feelings about the United States.

"When the United States invaded Vietnam in the 1960s, we in Sri Lanka watched with great concern and anger. Vietnam is a predominantly Buddhist country as is Sri Lanka and many of us began thinking that the invasion of Vietnam was partially an attempt of Christianity to destroy the Buddhist faith. So we became very vocal against the United States, its war against Vietnam and the possibility of the war to also come to Sri Lanka.

"When the war ended in Vietnam, the fears still remained, and as Sri Lanka was facing its own internal struggles, it was important to have an enemy which could stir up the people and unite them. Whenever you want change, it is good to have an enemy to unite people.

"Fear and misunderstanding of information were the biggest factors. That, along with the arrogance of many of the Americans coming to the country, stirred up and maintained the negative feelings. In truth we weren't against the people of America, but against the policy of the U.S. government which comes across as so aloof, insensitive and often very undemocratic.

"When the tsunami hit and we heard that U.S. military would be coming to help in recovery, we were extremely suspicious. Was this just another ploy to take over the country?

"But things have been very different. The American soldiers have been very helpful and friendly. Not only did they use their bulldozers to clear rubble, but they picked through the debris for unbroken bricks and other materials that could be used to reconstruct houses. They played with the children, bought food from the local vendors, and worked hard. When their task was completed, they all left.

"If that is how the U.S. military acted all over the world, they would certainly have a better reputation.

"So now I question my friends who are still anti-American. I tell them that perhaps we misunderstood too many things in the past, letting fear manipulate us and keep us from responding to global issues in a more positive and useful way.

"I still have a great distrust and dislike for U.S. policy in this region, especially their military aggression, but I've been able to see U.S. soldiers now as people and I need to make sure that my anger and suspicion is kept where it needs to be—on the policy of U.S. national leaders and not on individual Americans."

Kingman's reflection is not only an important message for the people of Sri Lanka but for us in America as well. We need to understand that anti-United States reactions by people in other countries have a cause. We may or may not agree with that cause and it may even be based on false assumptions in some cases, but if we can understand why people feel and react as they do, we can more readily find ways to resolve differences and break down walls.

My friend's reflection can also help us think about our own fears of others and recognize the importance of listening to information with a critical ear. Are misinformation and fear being used to try and convince us that other nations are a threat to us and our freedoms?

Walls are rising up between us and much of the rest of the world. Can we help bring those walls down by setting our fears aside, sincerely listening to others, maintaining a humble attitude and allowing God's compassionate love to heal our broken world?

—Max Ediger

Our economic challenge

Do not conform to the pattern of this world,
but be transformed by the renewing of your mind.
Then you will be able to test and approve
what God's will is—his good, pleasing and perfect will.

—Romans 12:2 (NIV)

As a young man, I lived on a farm and milked cows by hand. While processing the milk, one lesson I learned is that when we skim the cream off the milk, we can still make cheese out of what remains. This is a word picture for me of what is happening in our economic situation.

While some persons and programs have skimmed off a lot of cream, there is much that we can do with what we have left. We can downsize and live a more simple life. We don't need to try to get back up to the cream. We can live at a level of lesser demand, limit our spending, and share opportunities and resources with one another. Our greater success is not measured by climbing to some level of financial affluence, but by the quality of life and relationships.

For years we have preached that our American society is too materialistic, too affluent in comparison with developing countries, too consumer-oriented, and that we need to share with the needy.

Now is a good time for us to be salt and light in society in showing how to do just this. We have generally been a thrifty people; we have acquired resources by our ingenuity, and have moved up the economic scale in society. Yet we have continued to maintain a high level of stewardship, sharing through relief and hunger programs in giving to help those in need. Now our faith and practice are being put to the test.

The present global crisis calls us to identify in a very practical way with many in the world who have so little. They have had to "make cheese out of the skim milk" for a long time. It is our challenge to identify with the less affluent, to avoid a mentality that keeps trying to climb to the level of cream. We can be a voice for homogenization. Our society will be the better if the church maintains

Sarah Witter

its integrity. We are called to be salt and light, and salt is not food but retains its value in being salt, and light is not an object of achievement but an illumination that enables interpretation.

U.S. President Obama is working at corrections where some persons and programs have taken much of the country's resources. We applaud his efforts. But distribution to enable programs to provide jobs and to underwrite business ventures for enablement of our economy still calls for vision and ingenuity on the part of us citizens. My appeal is for us to practice the 'simple life', which we have largely lost; to seek styles of living that avoid the commercialization that too easily becomes competition.

I have a neighbor who has in a quiet way functioned as a one-man bank. He has personally loaned money, helped people in ways that were not condescending, and in it all he has lost very little and has gained many friends. Another neighbor, knowing well the plight of a needy neighbor, anonymously had her oil tank filled when she couldn't afford it. This is living the gospel in a style that I want to emulate.

This text has implications for our economic practices as much as other areas of life. We are called to a new, contemporary form of non-conformity that is not easy or simply cultural, but a style of selfless living that will express our love for others by finding creative ways for mutuality.

—*Myron S. Augsburger*

A space only God can fill

May God our Father himself and our Master Jesus clear the road to you!
And may the Master pour on the love so it fills your lives and
splashes over on everyone around you, just as it does from us to you.
May you be infused with strength and purity,
filled with confidence in the presence of God our Father
when our Master Jesus arrives with all his followers.

—1 Thessalonians 3:11-13 (The Message)

At the World Trade Organization meeting held in Hong Kong in December 2005, powerful and wealthy national leaders gathered to make decisions and policies that had a negative effect on many millions of common people all over the world. The workers who suffer most from these decisions and policies were given no space to voice their concerns or to offer alternatives.

They were shut out of a process that was advertised as democratic. How long can people suffer physically and psychologically before they lose hope in having their voices heard? How long before they decide that there is no longer space to talk and so they must take other actions?

I am reminded of a statement by Pat Schroeder, Colorado Congresswoman from 1973 to1996, "When men talk about defense, they always claim to be protecting women and children, but they never ask the women and children what they think."

When will our world leaders feel it necessary to provide space to those they claim to be helping, so they can express their own desires and options for economic, social, and political development?

Such events frustrate and anger us. Where is hope for a better world? I cannot believe that God created a world without hope. We simply must look for it. During the WTO meetings, I saw hope in the multitude of small, informal meetings taking place on the grounds of Victoria Park. People from different countries, ethnicities, occupations, faiths, and languages sat together to talk.

They began to understand each other better and to see the commonalities in their lives. Here in this "People's University" hope was as evident and as warm as the sun that washed over the grounds.

Simple farmers from countries in Asia, Africa, and Latin America expressed deep concern, not just for those who produce food but also for consumers who want healthy, safe food. Domestic workers discussed the issues of economic justice that touch the lives of working women all over the world. Factory workers shared the difficulties of caring properly for their families when their low wages are not nearly enough to cover food, housing, health, and educational needs.

These people came, not for political purposes, but to help all of us understand the injustices of the WTO policies in terms of human rights and dignity and to build a new world of justice. They are the expression of hope in our conflicted world, simply because they believe that a more just and peaceful world is possible. It is imperative that national leaders, as well as we ourselves, take the time to listen to them and take their message seriously.

When Nobel laureate Archbishop Desmond Tutu of South Africa spoke at a meeting in India, he concluded:

> "Even in hard-nosed, cynical cultures it is amazing that those we admire, indeed revere, are not the macho, the aggressive, the successful. No, the people we hold almost universally in high regard are such as a Mahatma Gandhi, the Dalai Lama, Mother Teresa, Martin Luther King Jr., Nelson Mandela; and why? Because they are good. We have internal antennae which home in on goodness, because you see, we are created for goodness, for love, for gentleness, for compassion, for sharing. We are almost the ultimate paradox—the finite created for the infinite. We are created by God, like God, for God. We have each a God hunger which only God can satisfy. We have a God-shaped space which only God can fill."

The WTO meetings ended much as people expected. Policies were quickly created that will most benefit the rich and powerful. Democracy was dealt another shattering blow as the voices the WTO representatives claimed to represent were kept so far away from the meeting venue that not even their largest banners could be seen or read.

Organizations like the WTO, World Bank, IMF and other globally influential institutions refuse to hear the voices of the people. Will violence be the only language those unheard, the poor and oppressed, are finally left with?

—Max Ediger

Jeanne Zimmerly Jantzi

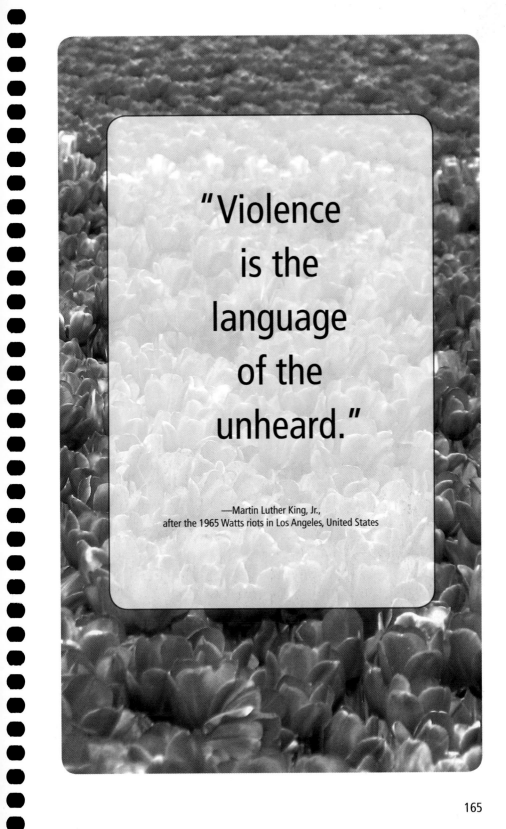

"Violence is the language of the unheard."

—Martin Luther King, Jr.,
after the 1965 Watts riots in Los Angeles, United States

Walking with wisdom in the paths of peace

Blessed is the man who finds wisdom…
Her ways are pleasant ways, and all her paths are peace.

—Proverbs 3:13, 17 (NIV)

Proverbs speaks of paths in the plural. What are the ways to the goal of shalom? What characterizes the actions that lead to peace? In answering this question, Jeremiah presents an illuminating case study in his conflict with the other prophets. It is striking that it was the 'false' prophets who were the prophets of peace!

"Oh, Lord God, look! The prophets are telling them that you said, 'You will not experience war or suffer famine. I will give you lasting peace and prosperity in this land'" (Jeremiah 14:13, NET).

At first Jeremiah thought God was misleading the people because of their message of shalom (Jeremiah 4:10; see also 6:14 and 8:11). Certainly his was a contrary message as God revealed to him the hopelessness of Judah's situation: "I will exterminate them by war, famine, and disease" (Jeremiah 14:12, Tanakh).

It is not surprising that Jeremiah, who proclaimed such a message of disaster and destruction, was accused of treason. His message was not in the national interest! He was weakening the hands of the people (Jeremiah 38:4). Rather than surge to the defense of Jerusalem, the people should seek to save their lives. Defeat was inevitable!

Jeremiah did not have only a negative message of judgment and ruin. He also pointed out the characteristics of the ways that led to peace.

In Jeremiah 22:1-5, Jeremiah is commanded by God to confront the king and to deliver the message entrusted to him. First comes the general command for 'right justice' (mishpat utsedaqah), the correct principles implemented in a way that brings about shalom.

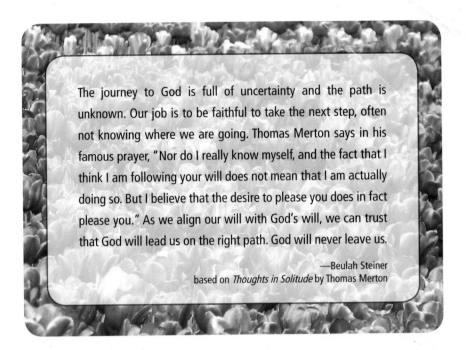

The journey to God is full of uncertainty and the path is unknown. Our job is to be faithful to take the next step, often not knowing where we are going. Thomas Merton says in his famous prayer, "Nor do I really know myself, and the fact that I think I am following your will does not mean that I am actually doing so. But I believe that the desire to please you does in fact please you." As we align our will with God's will, we can trust that God will lead us on the right path. God will never leave us.

—Beulah Steiner
based on *Thoughts in Solitude* by Thomas Merton

The king was commanded to pursue certain actions that illustrate what this would mean: …rescue from the defrauder him who is robbed; do not wrong the stranger, the fatherless, and the widow; commit no lawless act, and do not shed the blood of the innocent in this place (Jeremiah 22:3, Tanakh).

The litmus test of 'right justice' was defense of the weaker against the stronger—the protection of those who have lost their pensions, for example. Note the triad: the non-Israelite, the fatherless, and the widow. These represented the marginalized most vividly. In our context in 2011, we might ask, 'How are the homeless doing?' This is what the king was to supposed to be about. These were the criteria that measured the justice of the society.

Indeed, the very existence of the state rested on whether or not the king followed Jeremiah's instructions from God: "But if you do not heed these commands, I swear by Myself—declares the Lord—that this palace shall become a ruin" (Jeremiah 22:5, Tanakh).

God places before the king the path to life and well-being. He also places the alternative, the path to death, before him. Which of the two paths will the king choose?

The strength of a nation is not its ability to wage war, but it ability to pursue the well-being of its weakest members.

—*Perry Yoder*

Illogical

Do not deceive yourselves. If you think that you are wise in this age,
you should become fools so that you may become wise.

—I Corinthians 3:18 (NRSV)

We make three mistakes when we rely on logic and reason to present the gospel: We imply that belief in Christ is a logical matter, we assume that it is we ourselves who convert another to Christ, and we intimate that the power of God is not sufficient to do the job.

Christianity is not logical. Is it logical that God would come to earth in human form, as a baby born to poor parents, as a common carpenter, and as an itinerant preacher? Does it make sense that he would die a criminal's death to provide salvation from sin? Does it seem likely that, once dead, he would be raised to life? And what is logical about losing one's life to gain it; about being poor in spirit, mourning, or being gentle? And why feel blessed when others persecute you? If anything, Christianity is a religion of paradox, not logic.

People are not brought to faith in Jesus Christ by us, but by God. In John 15:5, Jesus tells his disciples, "apart from me you can do nothing." Paul says in I Corinthians 2:4-5, "My speech and my proclamation were not with plausible words of wisdom, but with a demonstration of the Spirit and of power, so that your faith might rest not on human wisdom but on the power of God." In his own time and in his own way God brings a person to the point of readiness, then guides us, as his agents, to present the gospel.

God's power is sufficient. Paul reminds us "For Christ did not send me to baptize but to proclaim the gospel, and not with eloquent wisdom, so that the cross of Christ might not be emptied of its power…" (I Corinthians 1:17). When we attempt to present the gospel cleverly, logically, reasonably, we ignore the power of the cross. We act as though the love of God demonstrated on the cross, and the power of God that raised Christ from the dead are not sufficient.

God's love, while not logical, is more than sufficient.

—*Tom Beutel*

Illogical action

1. Sit quietly during devotional time. Don't say anything to God; wait to see what God might say to you.
2. Be illogical today. Perform an act of kindness to someone who would least expect it.
3. Make a date to eat with a friend, neighbor or co-worker. Then pick up the tab!

Expectations

I have learned from teaching not to expect the logical of people. Students who were jocks become board members of the college! Students who were goof-offs become school principals. Our expectations of people are formed by our 'logical' expectations. As a general rule in teaching, we get what we expect.

I had the experience recently of going 'light' on the requirements for a course with four students, but 'heavy' on expectations. On the midterm exam the students graded their own exam in class, we discussed the answers, all did superior work and received an A. As a result of expectations and the ambitions of the students, all did a remarkable amount of learning. Let's replace our 'logical' expectation with trust!

—Perry Yoder

May 25

Someone loves you

"But I tell you, love your enemies and pray for those who persecute you."

—Matthew 5:44 (NIV)

A s I languidly lay in my own bed at home after days on the road and closed my eyes, daring traffic patterns and huge plates of rice, teeming bazaar shops and ancient mosques danced past. When I unpacked my suitcases, the smells of Iran wafted through the room—the dust, chicken kabobs, polluting traffic, pomegranates, pistachios and dates, the sweat of women, masked by perfumes and wearing scarves and long sleeves in 90-degree weather.

I was neither in Iran nor home. I was caught between an ancient and prideful civilization desperately wanting to be a respected part of the Islamic and world community only 30 years after its revolution and the familiar comforts of a society that threw off colonizing oppressors over 225 years ago.

I brought home piles of scarves, tablecloths and pillowcases, copper handpainted and enameled plates, sweets, pistachios (carefully irradiated at JFK airport), postcards, traditional manteaus, and heaps of unanswerable questions.

Throughout the trip, we had very little itinerary or sense of schedule or purpose. Often we felt more like a tourist group, appreciating ancient sites and Persian hospitality, rather than participating in a grassroots Fellowship of Reconciliation peace delegation.

This uncertainty was frustrating to us controlling U.S. citizens who wanted information and contacts to try to stop a war. Our last days consisted of waiting in the Tehran hotel for possible meetings, repeatedly eating in the same restaurant ("Anything on the menu I'm not tired of? How about the rost lion?" [sic]), and group confusion.

How does a peace delegation from *the* enemy country work for peace when we have no access to top politicians or religious leaders, when holding a sign on an Iranian street is nearly impossible?

Casual people-to-people contacts became ever more important. I had brought postcards of Orrville, Ohio, my home community, and "Pray for Peace,

Susan Mark Landis

Act for Peace" magnets, and distributed them freely. Recipients were delighted to receive a gift from the United States and amazed that my town was so small. Particularly, they looked at the magnet and said, "This is good. This is important. Your church is good. God bless you."

I searched for words that would translate easily my hope for peace between our countries.

I finally settled on, "Always remember that someone in the United States loves you," or "Teach your daughter that someone in the United States loves her."

In the poignancy of the moment, when I looked into someone's eyes and wondered if they would survive a 'surgical strike' near their city, 'love' was a promise to work for diplomacy and right relationships between our countries. For both of us, that statement put a face on the word enemy, a moment etched in memory of a desire to bridge the chasm of language, politics, and animosity.

—Susan Mark Landis

Action step

As you listen to the news, pray for the people whom your country calls enemy.

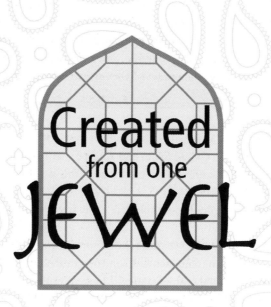

Created
from one
JEWEL

The human race is a single being
Created from one jewel.
If one member is struck all must feel the blow.
Only someone who cares for the pain of others
Can truly be called human.

—Saadi, Persian poet, circa 1200-1291

Cynthia Friesen Coyle

Lessons from Daniel

Although Daniel knew that the document had been signed,
he continued to go to his house, which had windows in its upper room
open towards Jerusalem, and to get down on his knees three times a day
to pray to his God and praise him, just as he had done previously.
The conspirators came and found Daniel praying and seeking mercy before his God.

—Daniel 6:10-11 (NRSV)

A pparently Gandhi admired Daniel. (As in "the lion's den and the fiery furnace" Daniel.) Gandhi admired Daniel's wisdom and nonviolent resistance to the empire ruled by King Nebuchadnezzar. In contemporary language, Daniel knew how "to speak truth to power."

In the beginning of the Old Testament book of Daniel, King Nebuchadnezzar has besieged Jerusalem, the capital of Judah, and thus begins the Babylonian occupation of Judah. The Israelite people are in exile in their own homeland.

The king, in Daniel 1, orders members of the Israelite royal family and others from nobility to live in his royal compound. These Israelites are considered the best and the brightest of their people and in turn, they are trained in the literature and language of the king. They also are instructed to eat the royal food and wine. We begin to see Daniel's wisdom and shrewdness as he and his friends refuse to eat the royal food. Daniel negotiates with his minders for a 10-day trial of eating his Israelite diet of vegetables while the non-Israelites continue with the royal meals. He suggests that the royal minders can then compare the Israelites with the others. Of course, Daniel and friends appear healthier than the others after the 10 days.

In Daniel 2, King Nebuchadnezzar has a deeply disturbing dream he wants to have interpreted. He calls on the wise men throughout Babylon for insight and meaning into the dream and no one could provide the king what he wanted. Furious, the king orders that all wise men be killed (verse 12). When the executioners arrive to kill Daniel and his colleagues, Daniel immediately "responded with prudence and discretion" to the chief executioner and began negotiating with the official to meet with the king. Daniel acts with both wisdom and prudence toward those in power to halt the killings.

Before Daniel meets with the king, he asks his colleagues to "seek mercy from the God of heaven" (verse 18). He asks his friends to pray while he goes to speak God's truth to the most powerful man in the land. After Daniel interprets the dream, he praises God "for wisdom and power" (verse 20).

By Daniel 5, King Nebuchadnezzar is gone; Belshazzar is now the king and he throws an enormous party for one thousand of his closest friends. After much drinking, Belshazzar orders his staff to bring the gold and silver vessels from the Jerusalem temple. As the king and the partygoers drink from these sacred objects, a hand appears and writes a message on the palace wall that no one can read. Once again, all the other wise men of the country are unable to help the king and once again, Daniel arrives to speak God's truth to power.

King Belshazzar offers Daniel purple clothing, gold chains, and third highest rank in the kingdom if Daniel can interpret the writing (verse 16). Wisely, Daniel refuses the gifts because he does not want to be beholden to the king, but he does interpret the writing. Belshazzar was dead by the following morning.

In these three stories, Daniel speaks truth to power through wisdom, discretion, and shrewdness. Daniel's interaction with the empire was almost universally of resistance. He resists the royal rations. He resists the order for his execution. He resists the king's offer of gifts for interpreting the writing on the wall.

The final story of Daniel's resistance toward the empire—and the inspiration for Gandhi—is in Daniel 6 when King Darius orders that everyone should pray to him for 30 days. In verse 10, "Although Daniel knew the document had been signed, he continued to go to his house, which had windows in its upper room open toward Jerusalem, and to get down on his knees three times a day to pray to his God." (Some versions have Daniel flinging open the windows to pray.) Daniel's resistance was flagrant civil disobedience toward the empire. This is what Gandhi saw as a model of nonviolent resistance toward occupying nations, toward the power.

With wisdom and shrewdness, Daniel repeatedly engaged with the empire powers but always acknowledged that God is the source of true wisdom and power. Daniel resisted the empire out of faithfulness to God and not out of self-interest. As people of faith, we too are called to engage the power of empire with wisdom and shrewdness and without fear while acknowledging the ultimate source of power.

—*June Mears Driedger and Kevin Driedger*

174

Now that our children are in their late teens and early 20s, it's fun to hear them banter about the trials and tribulations of being raised by peace-minded parents. They joke about the time I bought them "squirt dolphins" because I didn't want them pointing water pistols at each other. They get a lot of mileage about our family rule that you can only say "shut up" to the dog. They yarn on about when I helped them paint blue over the camouflage pencils they got free from the army recruiter at the fair. And how they learned to scale and eat even very tiny fish they caught while spearfishing so that one of God's creatures wasn't dying for no reason. Growing up thinking peace makes for good stories.

—Jeanne Zimmerly Jantzi

Making activism work

The mouths of the righteous utter wisdom,
and their tongues speak justice.
The law of their God is in their hearts; their steps do not slip.

—Psalm 37:30-31(NRSV)

For the word of the Lord is upright, and all his work is done in faithfulness.
He loves righteousness and justice; the earth is full of the steadfast love of the Lord.

—Psalm 33:4-5 (NRSV)

Learn to do good; seek justice, rescue the oppressed,
defend the orphan, plead for the widow.

—Isaiah 1:17 (NRSV)

Modern peace and justice activism seems to be struggling to make a difference. This should worry all who care about peace and justice, but it should be especially troubling for those whose social justice convictions come from a deeply held religious faith.

Indeed, acknowledging this reality does not mean the work of activists is pointless. On the contrary, a number of nonviolent campaigns have achieved tremendous success during the last century in opposing injustice throughout the world. Successful campaigns, such as Non-Cooperation against British rule in India, the American Civil Rights Movement, and the Solidarity Movement against the Soviet Union have repeatedly proven the power and possibility of nonviolent action.

But just as a lone soldier cannot win a war single-handedly, a lone peace-maker cannot enact societal change by herself. The most successful activism succeeds because of collective action—committed people speaking together with a message too urgent, too just, and too loud to be ignored.

Right now, peace and justice voices all too often go unheard.

Plenty of injustices are worth combating; poverty, racism, sexism, and ongoing violence in the Middle East are just a few. But attempts in the United States to protest or address these problems have grown stale. Marches on Washington have become routine and are often ignored. Protesters get themselves arrested on a regular basis, to little fanfare. And, for better or for worse, many modern injustices are subtler, less noticeable, and therefore less jarring to outside observers.

Additionally, peace and justice activists can sometimes hurt their causes by being unintentionally exclusive and unwelcoming. The very act of being part of a counter-cultural social group (often in an idealized 1960s mold) can become its own reward. To many outside observers, modern peace and justice activism seems defined more by this counter-culturalism than by the causes being addressed. People who are new to activism and do not "fit the mold" can be made to feel unwelcome, and are sometimes even treated suspiciously.

None of this is meant to dismiss the sincere (and important) work of peace and justice activists. Instead, it is meant as a challenge for those who feel strongly about peace and social justice issues to evaluate the causes for the lack of successful collective action in recent years.

In the spirit of this challenge, here are several suggestions for improving the effectiveness of modern activism:

1. **Reevaluate tactics.** The core strategy of successful nonviolent action—revealing injustice where it occurs while appealing to the better angels of human nature—will always be the same, but tactics must adapt to the times. Acts of civil disobedience that do not raise awareness of a clear injustice and achieve sympathetic media coverage can do little for their cause and are often counter-productive. One of Dr. Martin Luther King Jr.'s greatest gifts was his ability to organize vast numbers of people from different backgrounds, then utilize them strategically. Activism that does not do both of these things is doomed to fail.

2. **Use the Internet and other modern communications technologies effectively.** One reason the Civil Rights Movement achieved success was its creative use of the cutting-edge communications medium of its day: television. Similarly, modern activism must account for and utilize television, radio, the Internet, social networking, viral marketing, and other innovative ways of communicating with possible supporters.

3. **Reach out to those who are not yet onboard.** As important as well-organized activism is, activists alone cannot dictate when and how change happens; they succeed when they convince the rest of society of the truth and urgency of their cause. Activism is most effective when its message can persuade and appeal to people outside its core base of supporters.

These suggestions are broad and incomplete, and many other ideas can undoubtedly be put forth to strengthen the cause of peace and justice. Indeed, a major strength of collective action is its ability to draw on the knowledge and experience of so many different people from diverse backgrounds! But if those who are committed to making this world a more just and peaceful place wish to succeed, it is critical that they start by asking the right questions about their work and seeking the hard answers.

—Gabriel Schlabach

Skillet potatoes & peas

3-4 potatoes (scrubbed, unpeeled)
1 cup sugar snap peas (cut up)
2-3 tablespoons olive oil
2-3 green onions
Chopped fresh cilantro (or other fresh herb)
Grated cheese

Slice potatoes in home-fries style and fry in olive oil till almost tender. Add snap peas and green onions, stir and cook 1-2 minutes more. Sprinkle with cilantro and cheese and serve.

—Mary Meyer

May 28

Prayer for farmers

How beautiful on the mountains are the feet of those who bring good news,
who proclaim peace, who bring good tidings, who proclaim salvation,
who say to Zion, "Your God reigns!"

—Isaiah 52:7 (NIV)

Thank you, God, for farmers.
Help us to recognize the importance of those
    who participate in your creative work
    by growing and raising food.
We pray today for farm families
    who suffer from crises in the agricultural industry.
Help us to walk with those who must sell their products
    for less than the cost of production.
Help us to walk with those who face uncertainty
    because of disease and government restrictions.
Help us to walk with those who are burnt out
    because they must work both on and off the farm.
Help us walk with those who grapple with family responsibilities
    and difficult business decisions at the same time.
Help us to walk with those who have lost
    or fear the loss of their family farm.
Help us to walk with those who work from dawn to dusk
    and into darkness and yet cannot make ends meet.
God, help us to create a society where there is justice for farmers.

Amen.

—Carol Penner

Judith Ber Kulp

Powerful sharing

Then God said, "Let us make humankind in our image, according to our likeness;
and let them have dominion over the fish of the sea, and over the birds of the air,
and over the cattle, and over all the wild animals of the earth,
and over every creeping thing that creeps upon the earth."
So God created humankind in his image, in the image of God he created them;
male and female he created them. God blessed them…

—Genesis 1:26-28 (NRSV)

The responses to the difficult question quickly pointed out our different experiences. I was attending a Christian Peacemaker Teams anti-sexism workshop and had been asked to discuss this hypothetical situation: **A woman who serves with you on the Steering Committee comments that a man who also serves has touched her inappropriately several times and made comments with sexual innuendos. She has asked him to stop and he has not. What do you do?**

Yes, it was a hypothetical question. And yes, it was part of an exercise during a Christian Peacemaker Teams anti-sexism workshop, but I'm a 50-something woman who, frankly, did not want to attend. I know I've been discriminated against simply because of my gender and that I have been deeply hurt by attitudes and actions of men with power over me. I didn't want to relive the many incidents. I wasn't sure how to define sexism or its relationship to sexual harassment.

So, the question was uncomfortable. The compassionate, retired man I was paired with became indignant and immediately said, "I would confront that man, tell him his actions are unacceptable and that he must stop!"

The workshop began with worship. Then, women sat in a group and listed times they had experienced sexism. In a separate group, men listed times they had experienced male privilege. The females quickly had a long list. Many were fighting tears of remembrance. The men's list was created slowly and only with prompts from leaders.

Groups working against sexism define it differently. In general, sexism can

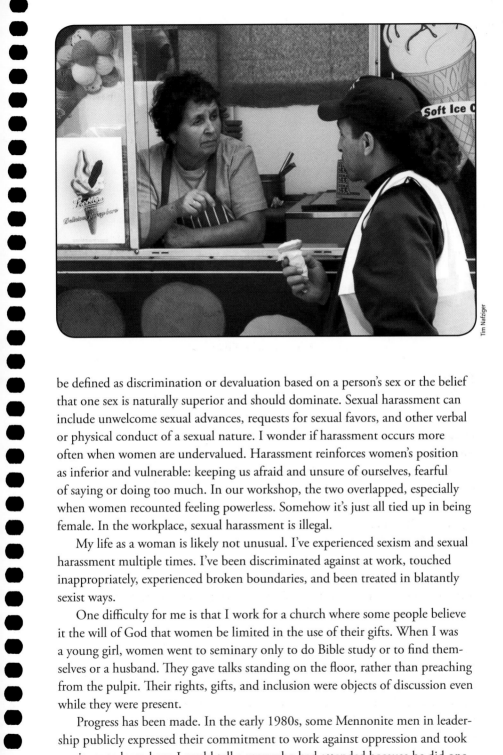

Tim Nafziger

be defined as discrimination or devaluation based on a person's sex or the belief that one sex is naturally superior and should dominate. Sexual harassment can include unwelcome sexual advances, requests for sexual favors, and other verbal or physical conduct of a sexual nature. I wonder if harassment occurs more often when women are undervalued. Harassment reinforces women's position as inferior and vulnerable: keeping us afraid and unsure of ourselves, fearful of saying or doing too much. In our workshop, the two overlapped, especially when women recounted feeling powerless. Somehow it's just all tied up in being female. In the workplace, sexual harassment is illegal.

My life as a woman is likely not unusual. I've experienced sexism and sexual harassment multiple times. I've been discriminated against at work, touched inappropriately, experienced broken boundaries, and been treated in blatantly sexist ways.

One difficulty for me is that I work for a church where some people believe it the will of God that women be limited in the use of their gifts. When I was a young girl, women went to seminary only to do Bible study or to find themselves or a husband. They gave talks standing on the floor, rather than preaching from the pulpit. Their rights, gifts, and inclusion were objects of discussion even while they were present.

Progress has been made. In the early 1980s, some Mennonite men in leadership publicly expressed their commitment to work against oppression and took seminars to learn how. I could tell a man who had attended because he did one-armed hugs only after asking permission, used inclusive language, and invited comments from females during meetings. My children grew up with a female pastor. However, when Mennonite Women USA organized a visioning consultation recently, the hot topic was the realization that far fewer women are in upper levels of Mennonite Church USA leadership than ten years ago. We also cried and prayed because women in our congregations are still abused by their pastors, but we don't have enough professional counselors to help them recover.

As I considered how I would respond to the hypothetical woman on the CPT Steering Committee who was experiencing unwanted attention, I wondered how to help her regain her sense of power.

"First I would invite the woman to list options she has considered," I told my workshop partner. "Then I might ask what she hoped the outcome would be. Together we could think of additional options and outcomes. Then I would ask her to choose what she wanted and whether she wanted to carry out the action alone, have me go with her, or ask someone else deal with the situation."

The man's eyes opened wide. "Oh, my! First you would *listen*!"

Men deciding to listen is the second most important thing they can do to confront sexism. The first is to admit it exists and they benefit from it. The third is to act—to learn about sexism and then to challenge it. (Yes, men are also oppressed by sexism and women also benefit.)

I'm one of the girls who asked her mom during church one Sunday why all the hymns were about men and got a lesson in grammar. (In English, I was told, men means all humans.) I still swallow hard when a man says 'sisters and brothers' because I feel respectfully included by being listed first. When I'm sitting in a meeting and a man says, "Men are dominating this conversation. Let's be quiet and invite other voices," I hear a small step toward inclusion. But I feel most a part of an inclusive church community when I see a man reading a book or taking a seminar and actively undoing sexism.

—*Susan Mark Landis*

182

Several years ago I bought a collection of assorted napkins from a thrift shop. They were a "collection" that I made by choosing all the mismatched napkins in a particular color palette. Having mismatched napkins is perfect for assigning a particular napkin to each individual family member, or to overnight guests, to use for an extended period of time—at least until it is actually soiled—rather than throwing away a paper napkin after every meal, whether used or not.

—Audrey Hindes DiPalma

Peacemaking with God in a world of evil and suffering

*This is the message we have heard from him and proclaim to you,
that God is light and in God there is no darkness at all…Beloved,
let us love one another, because love is from God;
everyone who loves is born of God and knows God.
Whoever does not love does not know God, for God is love.*

—1 John 1:5, 4:7-8 (NIV)

What if, in our being peacemakers, we are actually moving in direct partnership with the very Spirit of God, the loving Creator who wills that all creation flourish together in shalom?

The question of God's involvement in a world in which evil and suffering persist is one that continues to has riddle and trouble theologians and philosophers. The question is: How can a just God who is all-powerful and all-loving allow evil to persist? Even if God does not will or cause evil, the debate might suggest that a loving, powerful God would be capable of preventing it, and is therefore partially culpable for the destructive effects of violence and evil.

If a parent has the power to pull a child out of a busy street, but chooses not to, the parent is more a criminal than a loving guardian. In light of the violent devastations and injustices of the past century, atrocities that have led many to abandon faith in God, this remains perhaps *the* basic question for people of faith.

But what if we have misunderstood God's power? What if we have attributed to God a kind of power that is more a product of our own distorted imaginations than a product of God's self-revelation? We have imagined the nature of divine power to be such that it can alter, veto, intervene within, and overpower unfolding events of history. It's the kind of power we wish God would exercise and it's the kind of power many humans desire for themselves.

And what if we have misunderstood God's love? The most succinct and precise statement that we have regarding God's character is that three-word proclamation in 1 John, "God is love." This earth-shattering proposal, a revelation that comes about through the self-giving life of Jesus Christ, is still being worked out in our consciousness. It is not simply that God loves, that love is one of the things that God does, but that God *is* love. God is inherently relational and that relationship with creation and creature is always one of love. "In God there is no darkness at all," John also says. Not sometimes love and sometimes not love; sometimes light and sometimes darkness. God is love. In God there is no darkness at all.

God's creating of the world is non-coercive and always involves a partnership with the world. By its very nature, love presents itself as an invitation, a lure, a gift. Creation and creature, as co-creators with God, have a startling amount of freedom to dwell in or depart from the divine flow of love. God's power is not that which overpowers, but that which empowers through and toward love, the end of which is shalom, relational harmony in our ever evolving world. Not only does God not cause evil, but God's essence—the internal constraints of God's character, exclude the possibility of unilateral intervention.

If this is the case, then peacemakers are aligning themselves with the very nature of the creative Spirit of the universe. We open ourselves to the way of love, offering gifts that empower and build up. Through yieldedness to God, our lives become instruments of peace. What if this is the very thing toward which Christ calls us—to join in the death of our own notions of power and love, and receive resurrection power and love which has overcome the ways of evil?

—Joel Miller

Otterville   Merrill R. Miller

ACCORDING TO A 1995 U.N. REPORT HUMANS HAVE CAUSED THE EXTINCTION OF OVER 1100 SPECIES OF CREATURES AND PLANTS IN THE LAST 400 YEARS.

IN MODERN TIMES ALONE THE CAROLINA PARAKEET, STELLER'S SEA COW, THE PASSENGER PIGEON, AND OTHERS HAVE ALL GONE THE WAY OF THE DODO.

THE IRONY IS THAT HUMANS ARE THE ONLY ONES THAT CAN CHOOSE TO DO SOMETHING ABOUT IT.

May 31

Memorial Day reflection

Remember him—before the silver cord is severed, and the golden bowl is broken;
before the pitcher is shattered at the spring, and the wheel broken at the well,
and the dust returns to the ground it came from,
and the spirit returns to God who gave it.

—Ecclesiastes 12 (NIV)

My house is full of memorials. An ironing board, the quilt on my bed, a footstool, a hammer, a telephone, a clock that runs counter-clockwise, a microwave plate, and a drawing of a cat are among them. The only thing that these objects have in common is that they once belonged to people I loved who are no longer living.

Each thing has become part of the daily texture of our household, and they do often serve their intended purpose. Although I don't use my grandmother's ironing board as much as I should, Rosie's quilt is on our bed; the footstool that my grandmother Thelma recovered with vinyl gives me a seat at the kids' bath time; and the small hammer from my husband's grandpa Nelson is just the right size for small hands just learning and for hard-to-reach places.

But though they serve their purpose, these items are also hands-on reminders of the people who selected and used them. The antique telephone in my office frequently reminds me of my grandfather Oren's paneled study and I'm again the child pushing buttons and toggling levers. His backward clock on the mantel at home is a conversation piece. It allows me to tell the story of his passion for clocks and his amazing collection. And I am reminded of my grandmother Mary almost daily when her microwaveable plate and its plastic lid fall out of my bulging cupboard in much the same way it did at her house.

But perhaps even more important than the practical and emotional legacies of these common objects, is their spiritual contribution to our lives. The late priest, Henri Nouwen, suggested that "as we grow older we have more and more people to remember, people who have died before us. It is very important to remember those who have loved us and those we have loved. Remembering them means

Gloria Rhodes

letting their spirits inspire us in our daily lives. They can become part of our spiritual communities and gently help us as we make decisions on our journeys. Parents, spouses, children, and friends can become true spiritual companions after they have died. Sometimes they can become even more intimate to us after death than when they were with us in life."

One such spiritual companion for me is Lee, who created the cat on our living room wall. As a gifted artist, he inspired many with his insight and humor. When he died, our community lost not only a friend, but a spiritual guide: a man who helped us to walk with our questions about God. As I ponder the lines of that cat, I feel Lee's encouragement to continue asking my questions, to consider the nature of God, to appreciate others, and to reassure those around me of my love. Many other memorials in my house encourage me in the same way.

On this Memorial Day, I may just gather a few of the commonplace items around our home and tell their stories again to my children. Because as Nouwen said, "Remembering the dead is choosing their ongoing companionship." And I like having them around.

—*Gloria Rhodes*

June

Roses are red,
Violets are blue;
But they don't get around
Like the dandelions do.

—Slim Acres

In a Sri Lanka refugee camp the people live near the sea,
but have no fresh water.
They dig holes in the sand like this one, and as the water filters
into the hole, they scoop it out for cooking and washing.

Max Ediger

June 1

Living water

"…for I was hungry and you gave me food,
I was thirsty and you gave me something to drink,
I was a stranger and you welcomed me…"

—Matthew 25:35 (NRSV)

One billion people in the world lack adequate, clean water for drinking, bathing, washing clothes, irrigating crops, and other uses. Every day 10,000 to 20,000 children globally die from diarrhea, cholera, and other water-related diseases. While a person can live without food for weeks, without water they will die in a few days. Water is arguably the most important of all physical human needs.

Thinking of peacemaking as "making things as they ought to be" Perry Yoder, in *Shalom: The Bible's Word for Salvation, Justice & Peace,* speaks directly to this issue. Things are not "as they ought to be" when people do not have access to the clean water they need. Providing access along with the knowledge and tools to develop sustainable lifestyles in the face of disasters and other causes of water shortages are means of peacemaking.

Providing access to water implies both immediate relief and long-term trans-formation, which may include seeking to change unjust structures and systems. Our peacemaking activities can be direct, as in giving to relief and development organizations, or less direct, such as petitioning government and business leaders to change practices and policies.

Are we a part of the problem simply by the way we live? Usually our lifestyles are unconscious; we are just doing what most others in our communities are doing. By being aware of ways in which our lifestyles may be contributing to water shortage problems, we can make relatively simple changes in the way we live and be a part of the solution. For example, changing our water usage habits will help preserve and conserve this essential resource for the growing world population. By small steps we can bring big change; we can promote shalom.

—Tom Beutel

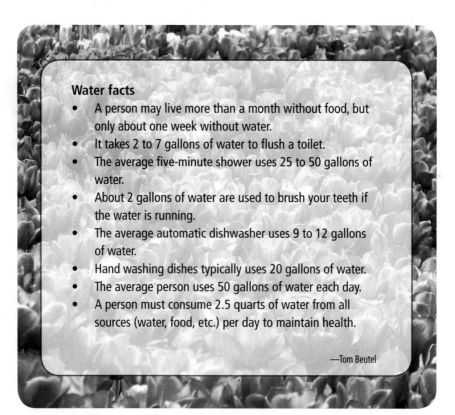

Water facts

- A person may live more than a month without food, but only about one week without water.
- It takes 2 to 7 gallons of water to flush a toilet.
- The average five-minute shower uses 25 to 50 gallons of water.
- About 2 gallons of water are used to brush your teeth if the water is running.
- The average automatic dishwasher uses 9 to 12 gallons of water.
- Hand washing dishes typically uses 20 gallons of water.
- The average person uses 50 gallons of water each day.
- A person must consume 2.5 quarts of water from all sources (water, food, etc.) per day to maintain health.

—Tom Beutel

Action steps

Save water

1. To use less water while showering, replace your showerhead with an ultra-low flow head that uses 1.6 gallons a minute, take shorter and fewer showers.
2. Choose plants that thrive in your climate's annual precipitation. When you water your garden, use a drip system, which is 20 percent more efficient than typical sprinkling.
3. It takes three gallons of water to produce one gallon of bottled water. (including the water to produce the bottle). Switch to tap water.

A visit with God

Jesus

As he came near and saw the city, he wept over it, saying,
"If you, even you, had only recognized on this day
the things that make for peace!"

—Luke 19:41-42a (NRSV)

I knocked on the door, it swung open, and there was God.
"Come in, come in, I'm so glad you came.
I was waiting for you.
The tea pot is hot and the muffins are still warm."

I followed into a warm, cozy sitting room with two soft chairs.
"Sit down...I'll be right back."
I sank into the chair.

God came back carrying a tray.
The small table between us held our mugs and muffins,
and after some small talk
God looked into my eyes and asked,
"How are you?"
"Burdened," I said.
"About what?"
"Stuff. Big stuff...like the shape of our world stuff."
"What do you see?" God asked.
"Some of us are filthy rich. Others of us are deathly poor,
and those in the middle are always complaining. Things like that...
and war and earthquakes and greed and...
We need help, God," I cried.
"What would you like me to do?" God asked.
"Well, for starters, spread out the resources better;
stop all the floods, tornadoes, earthquakes, and cyclones;

clean up the air and the rivers; eradicate diseases;
take care of the children; and stop the wars!
Stop the killing!
Please, make it all stop!"
There was a long silence.

"Do you have children?" God asked.
"Yes."
"Did you ever make them do something they didn't want to do?"
"Yes."
"Did it work?"
"No."
"It doesn't work for me either." God sighed.

Another silence.
"So what does work?" I asked.

"Love."
Tears rolled down God's face.
"And love hurts…I know."

—*Jane Hoober Peifer*

and now please join me in t

Prayer
Lord God, Almighty Lover of the Universe,
shape us by your love,
and grant us the grace to surrender to the way of love
so that your dream (and our dream) for this world
might be fulfilled.
In the name of Jesus whose way was and is love.
Amen.

—Jane Hoober Peifer

Oatmeal-flax seed muffins

Ingredients
1 cup rolled oats
1 cup buttermilk
1 cup all-purpose flour (or equal portions all-purpose and whole wheat)
1/2 teaspoon salt
1/2 teaspoon soda
1 1/2 teaspoon baking powder
1/2 cup melted butter or olive oil
1/2 cup brown sugar, firmly packed
2 tablespoons ground flax seed
1 egg, beaten

Directions
- Preheat oven to 350 ° F. and grease muffin tins.
- Combine oats and buttermilk. Soak for 30 minutes or longer.
- Sift flour with salt, soda, and baking powder.
- Add flax seed, shortening, brown sugar, and egg to oatmeal mixture
- Blend thoroughly.
- Stir dry ingredients into oatmeal/buttermilk mixture and mix only long enough to moisten.
- Spoon into greased muffin tins. Will fill 12 average-sized tins.
- Bake for 25 minutes or until brown.

—Judith Baer Kulp

Becoming an ally

"Blessed are the poor in spirit, for theirs is the kingdom of heaven.
Blessed are those who mourn, for they will be comforted.
Blessed are the meek, for they will inherit the earth.
Blessed are those who hunger and thirst for righteousness, for they will be filled.

—Matthew 5:3-6 (NIV)

We are straight, white men who benefit from a system that is racist, sexist, and heterosexist. We have learned well that we are against oppression. However, we've learned that living out this analysis in our lives is more challenging. In her book, *Becoming an Ally*, author Anne Bishop suggests a path for doing just that.

In understanding the concept of an ally, learning a new language can be a useful analogy. Linguists argue that the language we use to talk about the world shapes our perceptions of it. Likewise, learning to be an ally changes the way we view the world around us.

Becoming an ally calls us deeper into recognizing the way that all members of the dominant culture benefit from unearned privilege, just as those who aren't on the inside are oppressed.

Going deeper is about *naming*—that practice of unveiling a truer narration in the midst of an oppressive situation. Our sensitivity deepens to the way group power dynamics affect members of oppressed groups and we learn how to respond as an ally.

What does this *naming* look like? It means noticing and pointing out when members of the dominant culture are the only ones speaking in a mixed group. It means confessing those times when we've dismissed people because of our unintentional prejudices. It means honoring the moments when members of an oppressed group name oppression rather then getting defensive. It means making sure it isn't the women in a group who have to call out a man for making a sexist remark, intentional or not. It means breaking rank with other members of the dominant culture. It is risky.

I am my sister's keeper

I was lucky. I had a seat in the crowded New York terminal as I waited for a rain-delayed flight. Beside me, a woman hunched over, clutching her cell phone. "I just don't feel good," she rasped. "Don't think I should get on the plane." Overhearing her in our tight quarters, I asked if she'd like me to get a wheelchair so she could go change her ticket. "Please," she replied. I asked the ticket agent for a wheelchair. None arrived.

About 15 minutes later she was gasping into her phone, "I think I should go straight to the ER." This time, at a different desk, I looked at two agents and said, "The woman next to me is asking to go to the ER. Which of you is coming with me to help her?" The female sprang into action.

It took 40 minutes for oxygen to appear; a bit longer for the right-sized wheelchair to arrive. After the struggling woman left, I spoke to the agent who had overseen the rescue. "Forty minutes is an unacceptable response time. Will you promise to look into this, or shall I file a complaint?" I asked. She stammered a bit, but said, "You're right. I'll look into procedures."

It was only when the people around me, African-American like the ill woman, looked at me and said, "You're right! That was terrible!" that I wondered if racism had played a part. The woman in need was African-American. The responders were white. Had that made a difference?

—Susan Mark Landis

Naming happens when we bring hidden things to light, speak truth in the midst of error, or confess our complicity in systems that devalue others. No matter how nice we are, the impact of our words and actions can be very different from our intention.

Finally, being an ally involves a commitment to move past defensiveness when our own oppressive actions are challenged, as unintentional as they may be. If we are open to recognizing our own complicity in oppression, members of the dominant culture have a lot to gain, both socially and spiritually. Our relationships can deepen with those not part of the dominant culture. And when we are in deeper community with our brothers and sisters, we take a step closer to the vision of the beloved community and our liberation together.

—*Mark Van Steenwyk and Tim Nafziger*

Cynthia Friesen Coyle

Peacemaking in the kitchen

Alongside my trusty *More-with-Less Cookbook* sit six cookbooks from the Moosewood Restaurant in Ithaca, New York. Their recipes for nourishing and celebratory foods are a lot like peacemaking. Sometimes the recipes are simple. Sometimes they are a little more involved, but I have all of the ingredients on hand. Sometimes the recipe calls for something I have never heard of, and so I have to decide how much work I am willing to do. I wonder if the person who thought up the slogan "world peace begins at home" was thinking of his or her kitchen.

The recipe for Strawberry Chocodillas is a variation on a Cinco de Mayo treat from *Moosewood Restaurant Celebrates: Festive Meals for Holidays and Special Occasions.* This collection of recipes and menus invites us to expand our palettes to include tastes and traditions from all around the world. Extending our tables to include stories of liberation, reconciliation, and well-being symbolized by food is a form of peacemaking.

Because the historic peace church tradition does not place a high value on commemorating battles or wars like our civic calendar does, I prefer to think of these treats as a reminder of how rich, layered, and complex history is throughout las Americas, especially the southeast and southwest of what is known today as the United States of America. I recommend that you stop by your local library and check out copies of *Smart about Chocolate: A Sweet History* by Sandra Markle, illustrated by Charise Mericle Harper and *The First Strawberries*, retold by Joseph Bruchac, illustrated by Anna Vojtech.

—Malinda Berry

Strawberry chocodillas

Servings: 6

Ingredients
3 cups sun-ripened strawberries, sliced
1/2 teaspoon ground cinnamon
1/4 cup powdered sugar (divided 3 tablespoons and 1 tablespoon)
2 tablespoons to 1/4 cup orange juice
6 whole wheat flour tortillas (8-inch size)
vegetable oil
3/4 cup semi-sweet chocolate chips (divided into amounts of 2 tablespoons)

Directions
Mix the strawberries, cinnamon, 3 tablespoons powdered sugar, and orange juice together in a bowl. Let the mixture sit and begin to heat two large skillets with oil (cast iron works best).

When the skillets are hot but not smoking, place a tortilla in each and spread 1/2 cup of the strawberry mixture on half of each tortilla. Be sure to leave a 1/2-inch border. Next sprinkle 2 tablespoons of chocolate chips on the other half of each tortilla, leaving a 1 1/2-inch border.

When the chocolate has melted (about 2 minutes), fold the chocolaty side of each tortilla over the strawberry mixture, pressing the edges together with a spatula. Repeat this process until all the chocodillas are done. (It is a good idea to have a plate in a warm oven ready to keep the chocodillas until they are all ready.)

Sprinkle them with the remaining powdered sugar, serve immediately, and enjoy!

—Malinda Berry

Longing for greater care of all God's creation

The earth is the Lord's, and everything in it, the world, and all who live in it....

—Psalm 24:1 (NIV)

I write this during one of those spectacular spring days with perfect temperatures and low humidity. As I crested a hill on my morning bicycle ride, I could see for miles in every direction—the marvelous beauty of the fresh green trees contrasted with the crystal-clear blue sky. I could smell freshly mown hay, and the wind on my face felt like a sweet caress. My heart sang in praise to my Maker as I experienced the beauty of God's handiwork.

Yet as my eyes returned to the road, everywhere I looked there was evidence of human invasion of this lush garden. Trash littered nearly every foot of the roadside; pop cans of every brand in plastic and aluminum, remnants of fast-food establishments, discarded newspapers and magazines. The contrast between the beauty and the ugliness could not have been starker.

Isn't this contrast similar to our lives as Christians?

Action steps

Spring cleaning has been a ritual for as long as I can remember. Unnecessary items in attics, garages, basements, and other storage areas are sold in garage sales or given to thrift shops. Can we do the same with our minds and hearts this spring?

1. Can you change your desires when you fantasize about material items that are beyond your means?
2. Does worrying about retirement security actually change your situation? What could you do instead of worrying?

On the one hand we are made in God's image—reflecting the perfect beauty of God's creation.

On the other hand we have littered our souls with the trash of our human desires and wants—the ugliness of our sin. In order to "ascend the mountain of the Lord," we need to clean up the garbage of sin that obscures the beauty of what God wants us to be. When we have completed the garbage disposal, we can stand in God's holy place with clean hands and a pure heart.

—*Donald R. Clymer*

Prayer

O God, thank you for the beauty of your creation. Help us not to spoil with garbage either our environmental surroundings or the precious lives that you have given us. Amen.

"DON'T THROW GARBEGE HERE"

Max Ediger - from a road sign in India

Help in trouble

God is our refuge and strength, a very present help in trouble.
Therefore we will not fear, though the earth should change, though the mountains
shake in the heart of the sea; though its waters roar and foam, though the mountains
tremble with its tumult. There is a river whose streams make glad the city of God, the
holy habitation of the most high. God is in the midst of the city; it will not be moved;
God will help it when the morning dawns.

—Psalm 46:1-5 (NRSV)

The Psalmist must surely have seen his share of disasters. In these past ten years of living in Indonesia, our family has also witnessed firsthand the aftermath of the tsunami, two flash floods, two earthquakes, and a devastating volcano eruption. The disasters feel like a betrayal of God's good creation. The soothing ocean waves become a death force. The beautiful waterfall suddenly crashes and kills through the valley like a runaway freight train. The solid earth on which homes are built suddenly shakes and the walls that once protected now maim and destroy. The majestic mountain we climbed to see the sunrise erupts with sounds like war and clouds of hot gas annihilate all living things in their reach.

As a child in Sunday school, our teacher helped us to memorize Psalm 46. I remember her coaching us over several weeks. She demonstrated how to say the words "roar," "shake," and "tumult" with awful power. After the first lines, we paused for effect before going forward with words that were smooth as a balm in contrast, "There is a river whose streams make glad the city of God…God will help it when morning dawns."

Part of our work in Indonesia is disaster response. We often arrive soon after the horrible event to help with assessment. First comes stunned silence. It's hard to say anything past the lumps in our throats. And then we begin hearing people's stories of their experiences and losses. The stories become real when they didn't happen to an unnamed mass of people, but to the real persons we are sitting with. I let my heart go and share the sorrow. I listen and nod and write.

I tell the people that I am writing because others far away also care and want to know and share in their sorrow.

Sometimes the suffering people feel that a disastrous thing in some way is a punishment from God. Why would God allow God's beautiful creation to be used in such violent ways? Where was God when the flash flood swept through?

"God is our refuge and strength. A very present help in trouble." Where is God? God is with us. God is there through it and also when it's over to "help it when morning dawns."

In a disaster situation, it's hard to keep working administratively and thinking about the "big picture" when I would rather be working in a very personal way with the suffering people. At other times, the urgency of the needs— homes, trauma healing, food, schools—has felt so urgent that it seemed wrong to stop documenting, even to sleep. How can the weariness we feel possibly compare with the loss of family members, homes, and livelihoods?

I like to think that our disaster responses are like the river "whose streams make glad the city of God." My hope is that our actions for peace in disaster response be experienced by suffering people as God's presence—a balm in contrast to the tumult.

—*Jeanne Zimmerly Jantzi*

Judith Baer Kulp

Prayer for peace within

"...choose for yourselves this day whom you will serve,
whether the gods your ancestors served beyond the Euphrates,
or the gods of the Amorites,
in whose land you are living. But as for me and my household,
we will serve the LORD."

—Joshua 24:15 (NIV)

I have no peace. I am besieged!
For the temptations of my culture are in hot pursuit;
All day long they press their attack.
They pursue me day and night;
Their enticing voices beleaguer me.
I have no peace. I am besieged!
All day long they twist their words into wants and desires;
All their schemes are for my ruin.
They conspire, they lurk, they watch my steps, hoping to capture my life.
No peace within destroys peace without.
Be merciful to me, my God,
Help me in my distress!
I want no other gods before me.
I want you to be my master, to be my Lord.
Help me to find my peace in you.
Help me find the peace that passes all understanding;
Help me to be your peace.

Amen.

We are bombarded daily with messages from our culture, many openly recognizable but many so subtle that we are unconscious of their power to shape our thoughts and even our lives. Christians should be in a perpetual state of alert. It has always been this way, and will always be so. We don't deal with the gods of the Amorites today, but we deal with the gods of our culture who produce in us wants and wishes that put us at odds with God's kingdom. Our style of life in the overdeveloped world is unsustainable if we want justice and peace for all. The underdeveloped world sees more clearly than ever our lifestyle. They believe it's what they are missing and want a piece of the pie. Will we continue to defend our way of life when it is so clearly at odds with God's way? Can we calm the inner struggle to follow our culture and choose to serve the Lord? It is not possible to serve two masters.

—Donald R. Clymer

Tim Nafziger

"When you find peace within yourself,
you become the kind of person who can live at peace with others."
—Peace Pilgrim

A place of welcome

"...Today, salvation has come to this house,
because this man, too, is a son of Abraham."

—Luke 19:9 (NIV)

In Luke 19, Zacchaeus found an unexpected place of welcome when Jesus said he has come to seek out and save the lost. Jesus is meant for the lost. It is a lesson we have needed to learn over and over through the ages.

I saw this for myself on the High Cross at Castledermot, southwest of Dublin.

On this cross of about A.D. 1000 are a myriad symbols illustrating the life of Christ and the way of Jesus. Brother Eion, my guide, said the main purpose of the cross was to celebrate the evening liturgy, much as the early church has done since A.D. 400. I gathered with like-minded pilgrims around the cross in the neighboring community of Moone to worship in a similar manner.

"For my eyes have seen your salvation prepared in the sight of all people. A light to reveal you to the nations and the glory of your people Israel," we prayed.

In her book, *Sacred Space, Stations on a Celtic Way,* Margaret Silf says these standing Celtic crosses were the village's library, its pulpit, and its art gallery, just as they were the sentinels of the high places, watching over the community, focusing the people's gaze always to something beyond themselves.

I imagine these crosses also helped the wandering find welcome. They were "eternal bookmarks on the hilltops," says Silf, reminding "all travelers that their own small journeys were a part of the eternal journey of the whole human family."

Later that evening in downtown Dublin, I wandered into an old church as its community was celebrating Mass. "For you, my soul is thirsting," we sang. "May this be a house of prayer, a church for all people," the priest prayed.

A house of prayer for all people is becoming a recurring theme for me these days. May it not only be true when I am visiting in Scotland, Ireland, and Wales, but also in my home congregation in Goshen, Indiana, and in the churches and our communities throughout this land.

Jesus comes to seek out the lost like me.

Wouldn't it be great if our churches were a place of welcome for all wanderers?

—*Ron Byler*

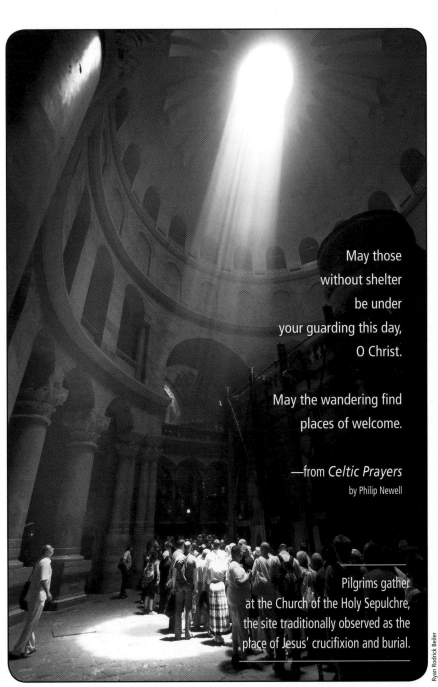

May those
without shelter
be under
your guarding this day,
O Christ.

May the wandering find
places of welcome.

—from *Celtic Prayers*
by Philip Newell

Pilgrims gather
at the Church of the Holy Sepulchre,
the site traditionally observed as the
place of Jesus' crucifixion and burial.

Ryan Rodrick Beiler

Seek peace and justice and have fun!

It's better to have a partner than go it alone.
Share the work, share the wealth.
And if one falls down, the other helps,
But if there's no one to help, tough!
Two in a bed warm each other.
Alone, you shiver all night.
By yourself you're unprotected.
With a friend you can face the worst.
Can you round up a third?
A three-stranded rope isn't easily snapped.

—Ecclesiastes 4:9-12 (The Message)

There is nothing like working towards justice and peace while having fun. How? I think of the times friends and I have "ganged up" on injustice and have done something together towards justice and peace. Of course, it could be seen as sacrificial! But it is also fun when what you are doing is done with people you love.

Recently my friend Jorge Vielman and I walked 75 miles on the Migrant Trail in the Sonoran desert in Arizona. Jorge and I have known each other since the late 1980s when we were both living in Alberta, Canada, and were recent immigrants from Guatemala. Now, twenty-something years later, we both found each other working for Mennonite Central Committee US, in positions where we can speak about the injustices that once made us immigrants. We decided to walk the Migrant Trail together this year in solidarity with our migrant brothers and sisters and bring attention to the deaths in the desert. It was sacrificial, but it was such a good experience to have solidarity between the two of us.

Almost three months after the experience, we sit over a cup of coffee and remember the experience. We can't forget the harshness of the desert and how

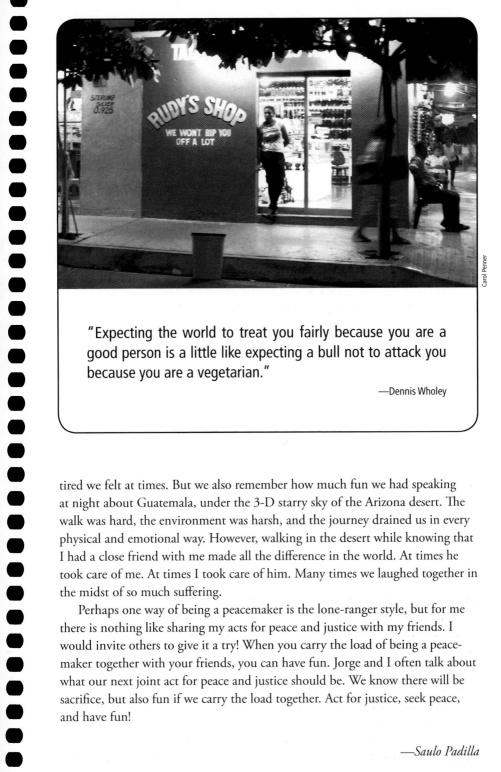

Carol Penner

"Expecting the world to treat you fairly because you are a good person is a little like expecting a bull not to attack you because you are a vegetarian."

—Dennis Wholey

tired we felt at times. But we also remember how much fun we had speaking at night about Guatemala, under the 3-D starry sky of the Arizona desert. The walk was hard, the environment was harsh, and the journey drained us in every physical and emotional way. However, walking in the desert while knowing that I had a close friend with me made all the difference in the world. At times he took care of me. At times I took care of him. Many times we laughed together in the midst of so much suffering.

Perhaps one way of being a peacemaker is the lone-ranger style, but for me there is nothing like sharing my acts for peace and justice with my friends. I would invite others to give it a try! When you carry the load of being a peacemaker together with your friends, you can have fun. Jorge and I often talk about what our next joint act for peace and justice should be. We know there will be sacrifice, but also fun if we carry the load together. Act for justice, seek peace, and have fun!

—*Saulo Padilla*

What we need

...there were no needy persons among them.
For from time to time those who owned land or houses sold them,
brought the money from the sales and put it at the apostles' feet,
and it was distributed to anyone who had need.

—Acts 4:34-35 (NIV)

O ne of the first pictures we have of the new church is that they shared everything so each would have enough, giving the world an idea what God's peace is. Justice is when everyone has what they need. God wants everyone to have enough.

When God invites the Israelites into the promised land, God explains the situation: there need be no poor people among you, for in the land the Lord your God is giving you to possess as your inheritance, he will richly bless you, if only you fully obey the Lord your God and are careful to follow all these commands I am giving you today (Deuteronomy 15:4-5 NIV).

The "commandment," of course, included caring for the needs of all.

The Bible often makes the connection between righteousness, justice, and sufficient life goods. These commands included Jubilee, a way to equalize the distribution of wealth every fifty years. As far as scholars can tell, this command was never practiced and there have always been people among us who don't have enough. Yet scientists tell us the world has enough food for everyone to have sufficient calories, up to at least 8 billion people. Hunger is caused primarily by human decisions. Unfair distribution, war, and governments keep many hungry.

As God pointed out in the Ten Commandments, our desire for the goods of other people leads to trouble, whether that be stealing, committing murder, or beginning a war.

Goods are so easy to come by legally in our society that we often do not link our acquisitions with these biblical ideals. Can we really be expected to make peace by comparing ourselves with those around the globe who have so much less? The biblical understanding of peace and justice says yes. We have a responsibility to remember that we are members of a global community in which we are the wealthiest members. It may be a tiny bit easier not to try to keep up with the Joneses if we are aware of the Khatoons, Carrascos, Duzdars, and Ouabas of the world.

—*Susan Mark Landis*

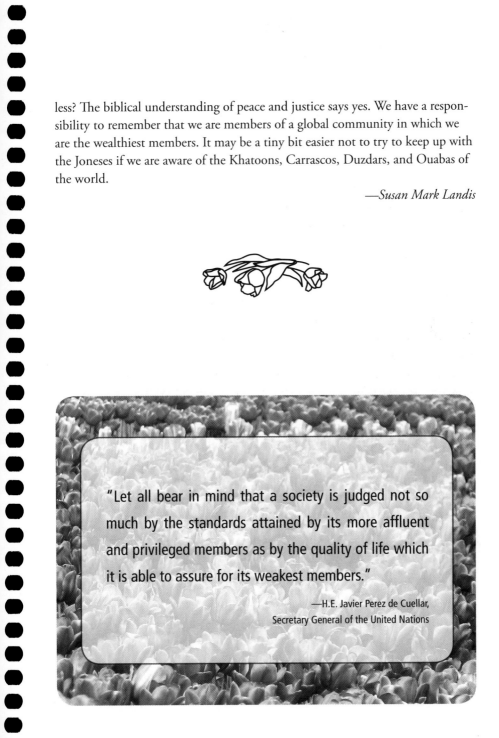

"Let all bear in mind that a society is judged not so much by the standards attained by its more affluent and privileged members as by the quality of life which it is able to assure for its weakest members."

—H.E. Javier Perez de Cuellar,
Secretary General of the United Nations

A way to conquer fear

"Do not fear, for I have redeemed you; I have called you by name, you are mine.
When you pass through the waters, I will be with you;
and through the rivers, they shall not overwhelm you…"

—Isaiah 43:1b-2a (NRSV)

Confession: I am a coward. I am ashamed to admit it, but there have been many times when fear has kept me from taking a risk for peace: fear of offending, fear of making enemies, fear of the unknown. I am often humbled by the courageous witness of others.

Several years ago I began to pray that God would help me conquer my fear. Honestly, I wasn't convinced that it would make a difference, but this is what Christians are supposed to do, right? Ask God to help overcome weaknesses.

One day, not long after I began praying this prayer, I went shopping at the small grocery store in the downtown neighborhood where we live. When I had made my purchases and stepped outside, I was confronted by a serious fight. An out-of-control young man, perhaps 20 years old, was screaming at his girlfriend. He was swearing, cursing, and calling her the worst of names. Raising his arms, he threatened to throw her to the sidewalk. At one point he hurled her bicycle onto the busy street, all the time carrying on his abusive tirade.

Several people had gathered to watch. If someone didn't intervene, the man would physically harm the young woman. Suddenly I found myself walking up to him. When I was right beside him, I heard myself asking, "Is something wrong? Can I help?" He turned and directed his invective against me. Only inches from my face, he raised his arm as if to throw me to the ground.

In the corner of my eye I noticed the young woman grab her bicycle off the street and start to move away. The boyfriend noticed too. He suddenly dropped his arm, stopped screaming, and quietly followed her up the street.

The crowd dispersed and I continued home with my groceries. I walked a full block before I realized that I had not been afraid.

—*Esther Epp-Tiessen*

"Prayer always thrusts one out into action sooner or later. One of its main functions is to induce one to think creatively; it stretches the imagination; it enables one to see things and people not as they are but as they might be."

—Muriel Lester, social reformer and pacifist (1883-1968)

Calm the raging of the nations

"For as the heavens are higher than the earth,
so are my ways higher than your ways and my thoughts than your thoughts."

—Isaiah 55:9 (NRSV)

God, who calms the wind and seas,
whose ways are higher than our ways,
and whose thoughts are higher than our thoughts,
Only you can calm the raging of the nations,
the impulse for war,
the eagerness to destroy another
in defense of our own interests.
Only you can take hearts of stone
and turn them into hearts of flesh.
And so we beg you to thwart the ways of policy makers
who rush to war.
Replace their desire for war with a desire for justice and for peace.
Give us the courage to be messengers in word and deed of your Good News,
to announce your reign to all peoples and nations,
to Congress and to our communities.
Hear the cries of those who suffer as a result of war—
civilians, soldiers, veterans, family members,
those whose schools and homes have been destroyed,
those whose souls have been torn apart.
Have mercy on them, O Lord.
May all of us together go out in joy and be led forth in peace,
people hand in hand with people, nations together with nations.

Amen.

—*Rachelle Lyndaker Schlabach*

Brown rice bread

In many years of living outside of North America, I have come to appreciate different kinds of food. Living far from home becomes much easier when we learn to eat and appreciate the foods that are available locally. We've learned to appreciate the simplicity of cooking the same thing for every meal, and we've learned to appreciate variety in other contexts. One of the standard pieces of equipment for expatriates living far from their home food culture is an "expatriate cookbook." Typewritten and photocopied, these little gems include collected recipes and kitchen hints. *My Babula Cookbook* from Congo has helpful recipes on how to sour your own cottage cheese from powdered milk, how to make pecan pie from peanuts, how to make pizza with pumpkin seeds or fried termites as toppings, and how to bake in a dutch oven over charcoal. Familiar food in a setting far from familiar can bring a lot of comfort.

Living in Indonesia, the comfort food that I miss most is whole wheat bread. Whole wheat isn't available here, so I developed my own recipe using brown rice to give me the brown bread I missed.

Dissolve 2 tablespoons yeast in 1/2 cup warm water.
In separate bowl, mix:
- 1/2 cup flour
- 1/2 cup palm sugar (or brown sugar)
- 1 tablespoon salt
- 2 tablespoons oil

Blend 3 cups cooked brown rice and 2 cups warm water.
Mix the yeast, flour, and rice mixtures.
Add 5-6 cups of flour.
Knead 5-10 minutes. Let rise. Punch down. Shape loaves, Let rise.

Bake in greased pans at 350 ° F. for 30-40 minutes.

—Jeanne Zimmerly Jantzi

Prayer for Pentecost

When the day of Pentecost had come, they were all together in one place.
And suddenly from heaven there came a sound like the rush of a violent wind,
and it filled the entire house where they were sitting.
Divided tongues, as of fire, appeared among them,
and a tongue rested on each of them.
All of them were filled with the Holy Spirit
and began to speak in other languages,
as the Spirit gave them ability.

—Acts 2:1-5 (NRSV)

Eternal God.
In this Pentecost season we once again open ourselves
    to tongues of fire that warm our souls and fill us with adoration
    for you and for your loving kindness.
We confess our complicity in a world and a culture that
    exploits the weak, ignores the hungry, and wages war over oil.
But we thank you for the gentle whisper of the Comforter,
    Your Spirit, come to bring us the peace and shalom
    Jesus first offered to his disciples.
And now, we ask for peace and shalom for our world.
Help our country to cherish the well-being of those countries
    against which we have sinned.
Help us to live as citizens first in your Kingdom,
Sisters and brothers to all who live on this planet today,
All who came before us and have passed on,
And all whom you have not yet created.

Amen.

—*Everett Thomas*

Tim Nafziger

The door is wide open

Then Peter began to speak to them,
"I truly understand that God shows no partiality... ."

—Acts 10:34 (NRSV)

Can you imagine? A military captain invites Peter to his home where Peter shares with him and his colleagues the good news of peace that Jesus was demonstrating all over Judea. Peter also tells these strangers that just a day earlier he had come to a new realization that God accepts everyone who believes, regardless of nationality. Imagine further! The non-Jewish captain and everyone else welcomes the Holy Spirit when it shows up! Hearing no objections, Peter signifies the momentous event by baptizing the "outsiders."

Of course, this gets back to other leaders in Jerusalem and Peter must explain himself. And then, in one of my favorite lines in all of scripture, Peter says, "So I ask you, if God gave the same exact gift to them as to us when we believed in the Master Jesus Christ, how could I object to God?"

Or as he says in the NRSV, "...who was I that I could hinder God?"

But we do, don't we? At least I do, over and over again, hinder God. I find myself protecting God for me and mine and refusing to believe that God is in the other, even when the spirit is clearly evident.

On the coming Pentecost Sunday, I want to remember the Acts 10 message: through Jesus Christ everything is being put back together again. And he's doing it everywhere, among every one. The door is wide open.

—*Ron Byler*

Rooted and growing in peace

*I pray that you may have the power to comprehend, with all the saints,
what is the breadth and length and height and depth, and to know the love of Christ
that surpasses knowledge, so that you may be filled with all the fullness of God.*

—Ephesians 3:18-19 (NRSV)

God, our source and our strength,
we offer our prayers for peace to you this day.
We long for your peace that is beyond our understanding
to take root and to grow in our hearts and our minds,
filling our entire being and spilling out into the world.

We offer ourselves to you, as a garden:
willing to turn over the soil of our hearts and minds,
welcoming seeds of peacemaking, receptive of your cleansing rains,
patient when growth is slow and unseen, persistent in times of drought,
attentive to digging deep to root out the weeds of despair, hatred, and fear.

We look to you to nurture and tend to the garden of our lives:
giving us courage and hope for new growth when life is turned upside down,
filling us with patience and persistence when peace seems elusive or absent,
working alongside us as we dig up the roots of the weeds that threaten
to choke new growth.

We give thanks that you are a creating and sustaining God,
that you are our source for transformation,
grounding us when we are unsure and afraid.
We commit ourselves to be people rooted in you,
growing daily in praying, speaking, and acting for peace,
sowing seeds that produce the fruit of peace and justice for all of creation.
Amen.

—*Tonya Ramer Wenger*

Carol Penner

Peacemaking through forgiving

Then Peter came and said to him,
"Lord, if another member of the church sins against me, how often should I forgive?
As many as seven times?" Jesus said to him,
'Not seven times, but, I tell you, seventy-seven times.'

—Matthew 18:21-22 (NRSV)

My local paper published a story about Reverend Johannes Christian, a man familiar with forgiveness. An adolescent boy threw a cannon-ball-sized rock off a freeway overpass, shattering the windshield of Christian's car as he drove past, blinding him and breaking nearly every bone in his face.

The boy pleaded guilty to throwing the rock and is now serving a 12-year prison sentence for attempted murder and vandalism.

Meanwhile, Christian has undergone a dozen surgeries with more to come to rebuild his face. Throughout the past year, doctors have reconstructed Christian's forehead, reset his jaw, and removed one of his eyes.

"I feel like Humpty Dumpty," Christian said in a monotone, the result of a trachea tube enabling him to breathe. Despite his physical pain, Christian believes he has to forgive the youth. The youth, Christian said, is like many of the 30 troubled foster children he cared for during the past 30 years. "He is a good person who made a bad decision."

His forgiving, compassionate heart is awe-inspiring. We know Jesus wants us to have a forgiving heart and to forgive those who harm us. We also know that a judging heart creates conflict while a forgiving heart creates peace. We also know, unfortunately, that it is much easier for us to judge others than to forgive them.

The apostle Paul asks us in the book of Romans, "Who are you to pass judgment on others?" Then he reminds us, "Only God can judge."

Judging others deludes us into thinking that we are like God—that we are all-knowing and all-wise. To judge another is to think ourselves superior. Instead, we need to cultivate a spirit of humility and forgiveness. We must acknowledge that

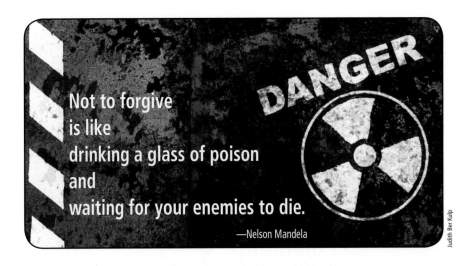

Not to forgive
is like
drinking a glass of poison
and
waiting for your enemies to die.

—Nelson Mandela

Judith Ber Kulp

we don't know everything about a person or a situation.

The parable in Matthew 18 is about a servant who owes the ruler an enormous debt. Rather than imprisoning the servant, the ruler forgives the debt. As this forgiven servant returns home, he sees another servant who owes him a small amount of money. The forgiven servant insists that he be repaid this small debt, even threatening imprisonment to the other servant. The forgiven servant cannot see that his situation is similar to the second servant's, and he is unable to show mercy as it was shown to him. The final verse of the parable makes it clear that forgiveness is a matter of the heart, a transformation of the soul.

The parable portrays the incredible kindness of God, who surprises us by not dealing with us on the scale of justice but by showing mercy. The parable invites us to view ourselves as forgiven debtors—living with and among other debtors. Because of God's forgiveness, our judging, critical spirits can be transformed into humble, forgiving spirits, creating peace around us—just like the Reverend Johannes Christian demonstrated toward the youth who harmed him.

At the youth's sentencing Christian told the youth, "It's my belief that there's no such thing as a bad kid." The youth wept and apologized to Christian.

They have since started a correspondence. The youth has written him several apologies, "He's really trying to turn his life around," Christian said. He has written to the youth to encourage him to change, and he will visit him in prison.

"I want him to understand that his life is valuable. He's just got a lot of growing up to do. He's got to come to grips with loving himself. I believe that somewhere down the line he can help people," Christian said. "Tied up in all of this is my healing. I feel better and the people around me feel better."

A forgiving heart creates peace. A forgiving heart creates peacemakers.

—*June Mears Driedger*

Kyrie for the city

"And seek the peace of the city
whither I have caused you to be carried away captives,
and pray unto the Lord for it: for in the peace thereof shall ye have peace."

—Jeremiah 29:7 (KJV)

At times we turn away
from the poverty we see,
from the jingle of change in cups.
God, have mercy.

At times we have no tears
when another youth is shot.
God, have mercy.

At times we long for an open field
and clear brook, instead of hard pavement
and tall buildings.
God, have mercy.

At times we long for silence,
as the sirens ring and trains clatter.
God, have mercy.

Grant us all we need
to seek the peace of the cities where you have sent us, Oh God.

Amen.

—Celeste Kennel-Shank

Masterful peacemakers

Whatever you have learned or received or heard from me,
or seen in me—put it into practice.
And the God of peace will be with you.

—Philippians 4:9 (NIV)

I learned how to barbecue meats by watching my dad. He would plan the menu, purchase the food, blend spices for the "rub," prepare the meat, get the wood ready for the fire, and finally, put it on to smoke. His smoked half-chicken was my favorite. I can still smell the smoke from the hickory or mesquite fire. He would begin the process hours before we were to sit down for the evening meal. Dad was a master griller/smoker.

Peacemaking activities also require thoughtful preparation and execution; to become a "seasoned" peacemaker is a challenge. There is no single recipe to follow, and bringing it all together is a slow process with many variables.

However, Paul reminds us that he modeled ways of being God's ambassadors of peace. God has been gracious to us and given us other people who exemplify the way of peace—people who are now members of the great cloud of witnesses like Gene Stoltzfus, Art Gish, Tom Fox, Elfrieda Dyck, Rosa Parks, Dorothy Day, and many other courageous men and women who modeled peacemaking.

Now it is our turn to "practice these things" by sharing our various recipes for peace. As we teach and learn from each other, I think we will hear voices from the past quietly echoing "Amen."

—*Richard "Dick" D. Davis*

Texas chicken halves (smoked)

Cut chickens in half (do not remove skin). Rub into chicken: salt, pepper, garlic powder, and Worcestershire sauce. Marinate for at least 1 hour.

Soak hickory or mesquite chips in water for 3 hours. Smoke in a charcoal grill or an electric smoker, using an indirect fire. Place a drip pan under the chicken and add water to keep the chicken moist while cooking.

Once the charcoal has caught and the grill is at temperature, place chicken over the drip pan, then add wood chips to the fire. Cooking time will depend on the fire's temperature but is usually about 1 1/2 hours (or cook to an internal 180 ° F.).

—Richard "Dick" D. Davis

Dump cake on the grill

Grease a 9" Dutch oven bottom and sides. Spread ingredients, as they are listed below, in the Dutch oven.

- 1 can (1 lb. 5 oz.) pie filling (Cherry or blueberry is best.)
- 1 can crushed pineapple with juice
- 1 box yellow or white cake mix
- 1/2 cup chopped nuts
- 2 sticks of butter or margarine, cut into small cubes

Place lid on the pot and bake approximately 40 minutes on hot grill.
Cake is more like cobbler than cake. Serve as dessert or as coffeecake for breakfast.

—Gloria Rhodes

Fellow citizens

So he came and proclaimed peace to you who were far off
and peace to those who were near; for through him,
both of us have access in one Spirit to the Father.
So then you are no longer strangers and aliens,
but you are citizens with the saints and also
members of the household of God.

—Ephesians 2:17-19 (NRSV)

One of my favorite peace images is a NASA photograph of the planet earth as seen from space. It is unlike our school maps that delineate each country with a different color to emphasize national borders. God did not create the world with borders. Those borderlines were colored in by human beings to differentiate one nation from another and to keep us apart. But through Christ, our cornerstone, God has called us all into one citizenship, with equal access to the Father through one Spirit. When I see the earth this way—an earth without borders—I imagine our joint citizenship in one Kingdom.

One of the most natural ways to work for peace is to intentionally break down the borders that separate people. We do this every time we make friends with people who are different from us.

As a child, I grew up in a very homogenous community. As an adult, I have come to appreciate how intentionally my parents provided opportunities for me to be a multicultural person even in that context.

I remember going with my parents to cross-cultural retreats and learning to enjoy Latino music. In 1968, in the heat of civil rights tensions, my parents took a church youth group to repair homes in an African American community in Mississippi. Over the years, my parents sought out people from other cultures living in our community and brought their friendship into our lives. They worked with the Overground Railroad in getting an El Salvadoran family through the United States to Canada. They participated in social action to persuade the U.S. government to grant a Ugandan friend political refugee status.

They welcomed more than 65 Lao refugees settling in our community through the sponsorship of our church.

During my childhood, my mother volunteered with a church service that filled in gaps in social services. Through these connections, she built a friendship with James, a disabled veteran in his sixties who struggled with alcoholism, and his mother, Lydie. James and Lydie scrabbled to survive in a crumbling home on the edge of town. Visiting often in their home with my mother, I learned to sit comfortably in the midst of smells and sights I had never experienced before. I learned to eat whatever I was offered and to say thank you for it.

After my father's retirement from teaching, my parents lived for seven years in Albania where they adapted once again and built deep friendships.

My parents modeled relationships of reciprocity and respect. I can't remember ever hearing my parents belittle the custom or practice of anyone's culture, race, or class. I saw my parents giving to and helping people of other cultures, but I also saw my parents receiving help from these friends. Lao friends provided hundreds of eggrolls as a gift for my wedding reception. Our family got garden produce from James and Lydie. Somphit, a Lao friend, sewed gifts of traditional clothing for my mother, which she wore with pride. During their time in Albania, Vali, an Albanian friend and neighbor, sometimes brought meals for my parents when they were tired from coping with few conveniences. I learned to value reciprocity and the dignity that comes from receiving as well as giving.

My family continues to live in places where we are surrounded by people who are different from us. We have the opportunity to break down the walls of prejudice and stereotypes that separate us.

This kind of change isn't accomplished through formal peace programs. It happens through personal relationships. Living vulnerably to both receive and to give builds trust and dismantles barriers.

Living with people of other nations and cultures, I have become more and more convinced that the kingdom of God should be my reference point rather than any earthly kingdom. I cannot get patriotic about a legal boundary. I get excited about the kingdom of God that welcomes diversity because God created it. This kingdom transcends boundaries and includes the entire planet.

—*Jeanne Zimmerly Jantzi*

What can peace and justice workers learn from sitcoms?

This is why I speak to them in parables:
"Though seeing, they do not see;
Though hearing, they do not hear or understand."

—Matthew 13:13 (NIV)

O ne of the most memorable episodes of the television show *Family Ties* I recall viewing during my childhood broached the not-so-humorous topic of home security. After the family's house was robbed, Steven Keaton, the father, purchased a revolver with which to defend his family. Over the course of a half-hour the family learned a gun was not the solution to their security paranoia, and rid themselves of it.

In sitcom circles, this popular plotline is called "Post Robbery Trauma" and has been utilized by *Ellen, Growing Pains, Golden Girls, Fresh Prince of Bel Air, Home Improvement,* and many others.

Likely due to a childhood spent in front of a television screen, my most efficient method of acquiring knowledge is the sitcom medium. It is predictable, mildly entertaining, and usually teaches a lesson (in stark contrast to much of television and film, which typically occupies itself with pulsating forth the Myth of Redemptive Violence).

I did some digging, and apparently *The Andy Griffith Show* and *The Beverly Hillbillies* were already being marketed this way—with study guides included— more than a decade ago. (Example: Andy and Barney lie to Aunt Bee about how delicious her pickles are, unknowingly setting themselves up to eat a dozen more quarts than they care to, ultimately learning about the dangers of lying.)

Almost every sitcom has a moral. That's why it's called a "Situation Comedy"; a mistake is made and hijinks ensue as the characters attempt to undo their misdeed(s). Looking beyond traditional sitcom plots to the genre itself, there are many ways sitcom tropes might be applied to peace and justice work.

The Aesop: Known to writers as the "Golden Moment," it is the point when the affected characters realize their mistakes and learn a lesson. I mention this sitcom standard only because it is a simple yet elegant manner of teaching. The tale of the Good Samaritan, the sower, and the rest of Christ's parables easily

Carol Penner

"God is a comedian
playing to an audience too afraid to laugh."
—Voltaire

fit this mold, and those who work for peace and justice should keep the strategy in mind when trying to get their point across.

The Fawlty Towers Plot: Perfected by John Cleese on British television, this device begins when one little lie is built upon by others before crashing down, typically culminating in an Aesop stressing the importance of sticking to the facts. The entire book of Jonah fits this, and even throws in slapstick for good measure. The contemporary approach to this plotline is the now-classic notion of taking two dates to the prom in an effort to keep both parties content. Juggling multiple causes is always tricky and makes focusing difficult, but we in peace and justice do it anyway in an effort to make everyone happy.

A Simple Plan: This trope is similar to *Fawlty Towers*, except it doesn't rely on a little white lie. A Simple Plan involves a supposedly straightforward operation often sparked by good intentions that somehow goes wrong, and characters go to ludicrous extremes to remedy the situation. This is the foundation of shows like *Frasier, Seinfeld*, and almost every Coen Brothers film; and is ideally avoided at all costs in real life. The lesson for the peace and justice worker? A project may appear simple, but that does not mean it will be easy. Keep in mind the comedic wackiness to which you could be subjected in exchange for simply rescheduling that meeting once again.

Those Rebellious Teenagers: A rebellious teenager is mandatory for inter-generational conflict. This is art mimicking life. Each generation of the church has asked "Whatever will happen to our children in this world without our help? The church is sliding precipitously towards the siren song of secularism!" Yet, we've managed to weather the centuries somewhat well. The energy youth can bring to the peace and justice movement is far more important than the energy spent worrying how they'll turn out.

Ugly Guy Hot Wife: Initiated by the 22-year chasm separating the ages of the actors playing Fred and Ethel on *I Love Lucy*, and carried on by Jackie Gleason, Fred Flintstone, Ray Romano, Drew Carey, Jim Belushi, George Lopez, Homer Simpson, Kevin James, and me. This trope instructs us always to be thankful for what resources we have, because we are lucky to have them.

—Tim Huber

Father's Day

Listen, children, to a father's instruction,
and be attentive, that you may gain insight;

—Proverbs 4:1 (NRSV)

How do we season 100-year-old holidays like Father's Day with peace? One way has been to take an anti-commercialization approach to our celebrations and keep things simple. But there is another alternative: we can, in our families, congregations, and friendships, take a closer look at what we believe fatherhood actually is from a Christian peacemaking point of view.

The historical development of Father's Day along with the latest data revealing how much more we spend on gifts for Mom compared to Dad show the weight we give to celebrating mothers compared to fathers.[1] Yet like the *pater familias* of ancient Rome, chieftains of tribe-based societies, or the commanding officers of a military, many cultures and groups base their hierarchies on males who community members regard as fathers. As we know, Christianity is not an exception to this pattern of patriarchy, "the rule of the father."

Hymn-writer and theologian Brian Wren has made important contributions to conversation about Christianity and patriarchy. His work includes hymns appearing in hymnals used by many denominations and *What Language Shall I Borrow?*, a book that invites men into the conversation about male- and masculine-dominated God language.

As a father himself, Wren asks us to consider a fact of life: "masculinity is a problem for Christian theology and ought to be felt as such."[2] MAWAKI, "masculinity as we know it," teaches all of us to equate manliness and fatherliness with keeping emotions, people, bodies, nature, ideas, and anything that is "feminine" under control. Wren observes that MAWAKI has condoned "male violence toward women, the recurring cult of toughness in political and economic life, and the irrationalities of the nuclear arms race." We Christians, he continues, are in danger of worshiping an idol in the form of masculine/male God-language instead of the true, triune God.[3] Read Wren's book to explore his recommendations for

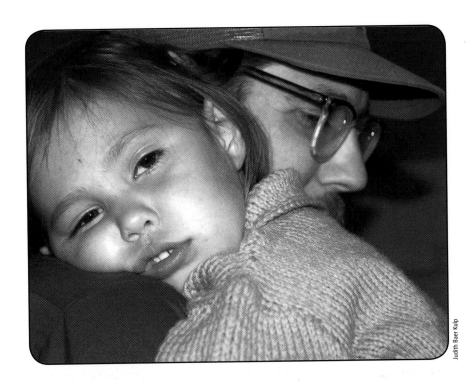

seeing and experiencing God in ways that open up pathways for men to understand their own masculinity.

I am grateful that my father has not considered his own masculinity to be something that makes him better than his mother, sisters, wife, daughters, or nieces. In fact, my dad has taught me important things about masculinity and Christian peacemaking.

When I was eight, my dad went back to school, adding a law degree to his doctorate in political science. I remember beholding my big, strong, invincible, college professor daddy utterly discouraged with himself because he hadn't done well on one of his exams. I learned an important lesson in that moment: grown-ups have feelings too.

As he began to practice law, I learned more lessons from my dad about the work he has done for the past 25 years to help provide for our family's well-being. Unlike most of his teaching at a Mennonite college, my father's law work has brought him face-to-face with people who do not share his Christian values, beliefs, and practices. The lessons he taught me from the lessons his clients and colleagues in the law world taught him have made me realize that very little of what happens on Earth is easily reduced to right and wrong, good and bad. On more than one occasion he told me, being a peacemaker is not very easy lest I think I could reduce complex political issues about war to a slogan on the t-shirts I wore with great passion and conviction. And it's true: doing "the right thing" is highly subjective. Loving your neighbor, your enemy, and even your friends is not for the faint of heart.

Being a daughter, my dad hasn't taught me any *direct* lessons about being a father. But what he has taught me *indirectly* is that a good and honorable father is a man who loves his children; finds life-giving meaning in his work; is not afraid to be honest about his foibles and limits; and most of all, desires to be a good, loving, and compassionate human being. As I consider my dad's life experiences including all the the choices he made, I believe that fatherhood woven together with a commitment to Christian peacemaking is marked by wisdom, patience, action, teaching, learning, and gentleness.

— *Malinda Elizabeth Berry*

---

[1] Most of us think of Mother's Day and Father's Day as U.S. American holidays, but nations and cultures all around the world honor parents in the late Spring and Summer months.

[2] Brian Wren, *What Language Shall I Borrow?: God-talk in Worship: A Male Response to Feminist Theology* (New York: The Crossroad Publishing Company, 1989), 11.

[3] Ibid., 12.

Blessing for parents

We pray today for a blessing on parents;
 single parents,
 two parents in one home,
 two parents in two homes,
 extended family caregivers,
 foster parents,
 and all who are in a parental role.
Give patience when love wears thin.
Give tenderness even in the face of anger.
Give clarity in the face of difficult decisions.
Where financial resources are stretched and anxiety reigns—
 bring relief.
Where there is estrangement and discord between parents
 or between parents and children—
 bring your peace.
Where illness and disability pose special challenges—
 bring renewed energy.
Dear Mother and Father of us all, inspire us with your love!

Amen.

—Carol Penner

My favorite childhood treat was graham crackers and milk. Here is my mother's recipe for homemade crackers. This is a great parent–child baking project that brings a lot of joy and satisfaction to all participants. It's a good way to teach math concepts, explain the difference in types of flours, where the flour comes from and how it is milled.

Graham crackers

Mix together and set aside:
2 cups whole wheat flour
1 cup all purpose flour
1 teaspoon baking powder
1/2 teaspoon baking soda
1/4 teaspoon salt

Cream together until fluffy:
1/2 cup shortening
3/4 cup light brown sugar

Combine:
1 teaspoon pure vanilla extract
1/4 cup milk

Alternately add flour mixture and milk and vanilla to the creamed mixture, mixing until all ingredients are combined. Chill dough overnight.

Divide chilled dough into thirds. Roll one portion at a time into a rectangle on a floured surface, returning the remaining dough to the refrigerator until you are ready to roll the next portion. Roll dough to a thickness of 1/4" or less. Use a pizza cutter or knife to cut dough into 2" squares and place on cookie sheet. Use a toothpick or fork to make holes in each square. Place on parchment-lined baking sheets. (Option: sprinkle lightly with cinnamon and sugar before baking for cinnamon graham crackers).

Bake at 350 ° F. for 10-12 minutes, until edges are crisp. Remove immediately from baking sheet and cool on racks.

—Recipe from Mary Helmuth, submitted by Carol Honderich

Judith Baer Kulp

Peace jar

At our house we have a peace jar filled with peace beads. Our two young daughters often have arguments and fights over toys, privileges, and what to play. We encourage them to find peaceful ways to work out the solution. The one who is the peacemaker puts a bead in the jar. Sometimes both girls make a compromise and they both put a bead in the jar. This helped us get through a rough time and the girls felt good about filling the jar with beads.

—Abbie Miller

Give us this day

"Pray then in this way:
'Our Father in heaven, hallowed be your name. Your kingdom come.
Your will be done, on earth as it is in heaven.
Give us this day our daily bread.
And forgive us our debts, as we also have forgiven our debtors.
And do not bring us to the time of trial,
but rescue us from the evil one.
For if you forgive others their trespasses, your heavenly Father will also forgive you;
but if you do not forgive others,
neither will your Father forgive your trespasses.'"

—Matthew 6:9-15 (NRSV)

God, All that is Holy, Creator of all that is good,

Open our eyes, ears, arms, hands, minds, hearts, and spirits so that we may learn
to more closely follow the example of Christ in life, death, and resurrection as we
seek to live your way of peace and justice.

Give us
Clear eyes to see others as you see them,
Sharp ears to hear your voice in the midst of chaos and imperfection,
Sturdy arms to enfold the wounded with your love,
And gentle hands to give rest to the weary.

Give us
Open minds willing to accept all those you send to us,
Strong hearts to faithfully follow where you lead us,
And willing spirits to fearlessly usher in your non-dominating system.

Amen./Mitakuye Oyasin.*

*Mitakuye Oyasin is the way prayers are ended in the Lakota language. It is similar to "amen" in English, however, the literal translation is "we are all related," with "we" being all of creation, seen and unseen. It implicitly indicates that as part of creation, we have privileges and obligations to God as well as to God's entire creation in a complex web of relationships, not unlike a family. Upholding such familial obligations is what justice and peace look like.

—Patricia Burdette

Judith Baer Kulp

Tree prayer

The person is like a tree planted by streams of water,
which yields its fruit in season
and whose leaf does not wither—whatever they do prospers.

Psalm 1:3 (NIV)

Help us to learn from the trees to be your people.

Like the strong oak with its deep roots,
establish us in your word, in community, in prayer.

Like the graceful willow bending in the wind,
strengthen us to withstand tumults and trials.

Like the tall jack pine, true and straight,
make us be pure and single-minded, always looking to you.

Like the rustling poplar, with shiny shimmering leaves,
give us joy in the winds of life.

Like the stately sycamore lining smoggy city streets,
empower us to grow where we are planted, regardless of conditions.

Like the delicate peach tree,
make us fruitful and sweet in the lives of those around us.

Like the aromatic cedar, evergreen in hard seasons,
allow us to produce the fragrance of mercy even when we are broken.

Remembering the tree of Calvary,
teach us the value of taking up our cross daily in service for others.

—Carol Penner

Drawing trees

Fruit trees of all kinds will grow on both banks of the river.
Their leaves will not wither, nor will their fruit fail.
Every month they will bear,
because the water from the sanctuary flows to them.
Their fruit will serve for food and their leaves for healing.

—Ezekiel 47:12 (NIV)

This week I participated in STAR, or Strategies for Trauma Awareness and Resilience, a workshop offered by the Center for Justice and Peacebuilding at Eastern Mennonite University (EMU). I was familiar with STAR, and I was eager to learn more about trauma and its physical, emotional, and spiritual effects and its linkages to violence.

I am familiar with STAR because I also teach at EMU. And while teaching is fulfilling to me, my subject matter is intense, and sometimes even painful. I teach about conflict, violence, and injustice. I also teach about how to build peace, and the great capacity that humans have to love and do good in the world. However, like social workers, police officers, humanitarian assistance workers, fire fighters, military personnel, and others, my occupation of teaching about conflict and violence forces me to look directly at human suffering caused by human cruelty. My subject area exposes me and my students to realities that produce strong feelings that are often difficult to process.

Over time, I've become sensitive to these stories of human suffering. I have begun to avoid TV journalism, movies, and anything I fear will contain more violence. Witnessing violence in videos I use in classes, for example, has begun to affect me in the same way that witnessing violence or trauma first-hand affects any of us—through physical responses in the body. The physical response I feel in the pit of my stomach when I encounter more suffering is a trauma response—even when caused by indirect or vicarious experiences of trauma.

The traumas we experience are different for everyone. For some, a life-threatening illness, the loss of someone close, or a dangerous situation can cause trauma, but what causes trauma is different for each of us, and for some of us, the trauma may even be caused by something that others might see as trivial. But the physical response is real. It is the body's response to being overwhelmed.

However we experience trauma, whether directly or vicariously, our body attempts to respond by preparing us to physically deal with the threat. These physiological responses prepare us to fight, to run (flight), and sometimes to freeze. When freezing happens, the trauma energy gets trapped in our bodies and we may use that energy to act in self-damaging ways—risky behaviors, alcohol, drugs, depression, cutting—or to act out (through violence against others—child abuse, aggressive behavior, direct physical violence, and emotional violence).

These cycles of violence against self and others are prevalent in our society, and examples can be found at personal, community, national, and international levels. But these cycles can be broken, and it was my interest in learning more about breaking cycles of violence and learning strategies for trauma resilience that led me to STAR.

The personal traumas shared about in class were difficult to hear. Some were so painful that we shared only silence and tears. In my unfamiliar role as student, sitting at a table, I found it difficult to still my body and I sought acceptable ways to deal with the trauma energy. I used the play dough, coloring sheets, and colored pencils provided by the STAR facilitators, and I enjoyed the massage and yoga options provided, but I was still distracted and tense.

Finally on day three, I started to draw. I drew and drew and drew. By the end of the week, I realized that most of my drawings were from nature…a tree branch, a bowl of fruit, flowers of every shape and size. But all week, most of all, I had been drawing trees; branches, leaves of many colors and shapes, different types of trees, and finally a tree with a gnarled knot in the center, a memory of a tree that stands in my backyard. Ten years ago, we had caused it trauma by cutting off a branch about 18 inches in diameter and it has been very slowly growing over the damage. Today when I looked at the tree, I realized the scar had shrunk to only several inches wide. The tree has remained healthy on the outside while bearing and healing that injury.

Just like my own traumas and the experiences of trauma of each of the participants in our classroom, the tree in my yard has been repairing the injury. And though the tree has been resilient, healing has taken time. The hopeful message of STAR is that like trees, humans are resilient too, and we can learn strategies that help our bodies through the healing process and out of the cycles of violence in which we get trapped.

For me, the process of going through STAR, crying with others, telling my story, and drawing trees has helped moved me further along my own path to healing. I'm still avoiding TV, but I've been able to talk about some of my past traumas without the familiar physical responses (a sign that the trauma energy has been sufficiently processed to pass on out of my body). And I'm at peace as I think about teaching again in the fall.

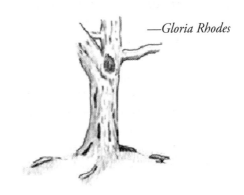

—*Gloria Rhodes*

Otterville   Merrill R. Miller

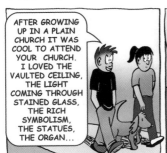

AFTER GROWING UP IN A PLAIN CHURCH IT WAS COOL TO ATTEND YOUR CHURCH. I LOVED THE VAULTED CEILING, THE LIGHT COMING THROUGH STAINED GLASS, THE RICH SYMBOLISM, THE STATUES, THE ORGAN...

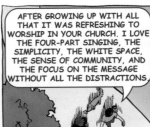

AFTER GROWING UP WITH ALL THAT IT WAS REFRESHING TO WORSHIP IN YOUR CHURCH. I LOVE THE FOUR-PART SINGING, THE SIMPLICITY, THE WHITE SPACE, THE SENSE OF COMMUNITY, AND THE FOCUS ON THE MESSAGE WITHOUT ALL THE DISTRACTIONS.

I STILL PREFER WORSHIPPING OUTDOORS!

AMEN

Frittata

Ingredients
8 eggs
Shredded cheese
Assorted leftovers (cooked veggies and/or meat)
Bread, cut in cubes

Directions
- Preheat oven to 400 ° F.
- Break eggs into mixing bowl. Beat well. Salt and pepper to taste
- Add shredded cheese. Mix well.
- Heat skillet over medium heat. Add 2 tablespoons of fat (butter & olive oil combined is my favorite) A nonstick skillet makes slicing and serving effortless, but a regular one works, too.
- When fat is hot, add filling (bread, cooked veggies, meat). Heat through
- Pour in egg mixture. Let it set a few seconds, just until edges start to firm up. Run a rubber spatula along the edge of the frittata, lifting and pushing filling around to let liquid egg flow underneath.
- Repeat 2 or 3 times until most of the liquid has set.
- Place skillet (ovenproof only!) in oven for 10-15 minutes, just until all egg mixture has completely set. If using nonstick skillet, slide onto plate or pie pan to cut and serve.

—Audrey Hindes DiPalma

June 23

Migrant trail reflection

Is not this the fast that I choose: to loose the bonds of injustice,
to undo the thongs of the yoke,
to let the oppressed go free, and to break every yoke?
Is it not to share your bread with the hungry,
and bring the homeless poor into your house; when you see the naked, to cover them,
and not to hide yourself from your own kin?
Then your light shall break forth like the dawn, and your healing shall spring up
quickly; your vindicator shall go before you,
the glory of the LORD shall be your rearguard.

—Isaiah 58:6-8 (NRSV)

Seven days on the Migrant Trail, walking 75 miles in the desert to remember people who have died, exhausts me emotionally and physically. The experience is also life-changing. I pray more during the Migrant Trail than any other time of the year.

For several hours each day, I walk in silence to pray for Ricarda Macedo Zaragosa, a 53-year-old woman from Mexico, found dead on May 26, 2005 in Yuma, Arizona. Ricarda died of exposure and heat exhaustion. As I carry the cross with Ricarda's name, I pray that her family would know that she was being remembered and honored. I pray that the death she died would not be repeated by others. Sadly, I know it will.

I prayed for Santos' family from Honduras, his wife Esperanza, and their two children. I thought of Mark and Lynne Baker, Mennonite Brethren professors in Fresno and close family friends of Santos. Santos was lost/disappeared and is presumed dead somewhere in the state of Texas. I prayed that Santos' children would find comfort in their daily living despite the absence of their father.

I prayed for the people who were walking through the desert as we were walking. I couldn't see them but I knew they were there. We saw a group of men with backpacks before we left Sasabe, Sonora. I prayed that they would find access to water and didn't have to walk too long or get too many blisters.

I prayed for the policymakers in Washington, DC to see the human impact of deadly policies that force people into the harsh desert instead of allowing them to pass through ports of entry.

I don't think that I prayed for the migrant we encountered along Highway 286. When we came upon Juan, we stopped to offer water and to see if he needed medical attention or assistance. Christie, another walker from Michigan, and I were returning from picking up the portable toilets when we saw him walking on the road. Juan had dozens of cuts from spines of cactus on his face and arms. He asked for a ride, which I promptly indicated was not possible. He asked to borrow a phone, which I granted him. Christie and I handed him all the water we had. After ten minutes of saying no to his repeated requests for a ride, I requested the return of the phone but Juan was not ready to return it. After a few more minutes, Juan ran off.

While I didn't pray for Juan in this instance, I do hope that he arrived to his destination safely. I felt kind of foolish for losing my phone. And yet, upon further reflection of the Biblical command to provide water for the thirsty, food for the hungry, and liberation for the oppressed, I knew I would do the same thing again. And then I wondered if sharing my phone was kind of like what Paul in the book of 2 Corinthians called foolishness for Christ?

Could it be that the power of the Gospel, the power of radical change is evident in simple gifts of water bottles and cell phones offered to those in need? What radical change could happen as a result of thousands of God's children providing for others in the desert?

The Migrant Trail is my prayer walk.

It is a time to remember individuals, a time to remember the impact of government policies, a time to renew my commitment to care for individuals and to work toward policy change.

—Jodi Read

246

Anton Flores

Wall at the border between Arizona and Mexico

Guide our feet into the way of peace

Then his father Zechariah was filled with the Holy Spirit and spoke this prophecy:
"Blessed be the Lord God of Israel,
for he has looked favorably on his people and redeemed them.
He has raised up a mighty savior* for us
in the house of his servant David,
as he spoke through the mouth of his holy prophets from of old,
that we would be saved from our enemies and from the hand of all who hate us."

—Luke 1:67-79 (NRSV)

O n June 24, much of God's church commemorates the Feast of the Nativity of John the Baptist, and that has given me extra reason to contemplate the legacy of the Baptist. I say "extra reason" because we monks hold St. John the Baptist in a very special place in our hearts. The Baptist, of course, was the great forerunner of Jesus the Christ and, as such, called people to a life of simplicity and conversion.

That is a call that all monastics attempt to live into each day.

It is a call that many Christians respond to quite deeply as they live into their particular vocations.

Each morning here in the monastery, and in most throughout the world, the "Benedictus" is prayed toward the end of our morning Office (the recitation of the psalms and other prayers from the Scriptures).

The Benedictus is the Latin word for the prayer/prophecy that John's father, Zechariah, proclaims at his birth. This is taken from Luke 1:67-79 in which Zechariah, "filled with the Holy Spirit" speaks a "prophecy" that begins: "Blessed be the Lord God of Israel." In the first section of the prayer, Zechariah addresses himself to God. The second section contains the prophecy, beginning with verse 76, where Zechariah addresses himself directly to the newborn John. The translation we use reads as follows:

Guide our feet
into the
way of peace.

Jonathan Dyck

And you child shall be called the prophet of the Most High
for you will go before the Lord to prepare the way
to give God's people knowledge of salvation
by the forgiveness of their sins.
In the tender compassion of our God,
the dawn from on High shall break upon us.
To shine on those who dwell in darkness and the shadow of death,
and to guide our feet into the way of peace.

While Zechariah was speaking of his newly born child, John, it has always seemed to me that this prophecy was a call to all of us to "prepare the way" for the Most High. By our life, our prayer, and our work, we are to give knowledge of God's salvation to all of God's people by, in part, forgiving their sins. The Baptist is remembered for his call to repentance. And yes, we should remind people of their need to repent when appropriate. But it occurs to me that in order to model the "tender compassion of our God" we ought to be in the business of repenting ourselves and of forgiving others of their sins.

Those sins might be of a personal nature—anything from petty hurts and slights to major breaches of relationship. They might also be sins committed on a more global scale. Our world dwells in the darkness of religious zealotry of all types. What if we were to allow "the dawn to break upon us" by forgiving those we deem to be religious zealots, for example? Imagine a peaceful revolution—on a global scale—that we could begin to engage in before the sun goes down. What would that forgiveness look like?

Forgiveness, remember, is not a feeling. It is an action. It is making a conscious effort to release any anger, animosity and hatred in our hearts toward a particular person or people; it is not wishing them harm. It is making an effort to open lines of communication with them in order to foster dialogue and to discover what commonalities of belief and practice might be found. It is not glossing over our differences, rather it is finding a way to speak our truth in a manner that is loving and compassionate. It is, ultimately, the practice of enormous patience; it is praying and hoping for their well-being.

Perhaps this month, in memory of St. John the Baptist, each of us can find it in our hearts to forgive a religious zealot—or at least someone that we think is a religious zealot. Keep in mind that the Baptist was murdered because he was thought to be a religious zealot. Zealots come in all forms—every religious tradition has them and we ought not allow zealotry to control the global dialogue around issues of faith, non-violence, and peace. People we assume to be zealots live in our own neighborhoods as well as half way around the world. Is there someone, or some church, synagogue, mosque, or some other group that you view with great suspicion or fear, that you or your church can reach out to in order to begin the process of conversion which, most likely, both you and they need? Don't you think that would open us to allow God to "guide our feet into the way of peace?"

Pax.

—*Brother James Dowd*

Liberate us, O God

I am the Lord your God, who has freed you from the burdens of the Egyptians.
—Exodus 6:7 (NRSV)

God of steadfast love, you liberate your people from slavery.
Hear our prayer as we pray in the heart of empire.

We pray for those tied to their treasures on earth.
Here in this land of riches,
liberate us from the temptations, tightfistedness, and unsustainable lifestyles
that regularly beckon us.

We pray for those who mar creation.
Here in this land of choked highways, despoiled seas, and warming climate,
liberate us from our addiction to oil.

We pray for those who resort to violence.
Here is this land of women's shelters, gun shops, and traumatized soldiers,
liberate us from our misplaced faith in might.

We pray for those who devalue other people.
Here in this land where many are quick to discriminate, deport, and exclude,
liberate us from our fear-filled judgments.

Liberate us, O God, to new lands of promise.
Feed us with the bread of imagination and the water of courage to sustain us
in the wilderness.
Guide us from complacency and complicity to your holy mountain.
For you shall be our God and we shall be your people.
Amen.

—Karl S. Shelly

Are you my neighbor?

On one occasion an expert in the law stood up to test Jesus.
"Teacher," he asked, "what must I do to inherit eternal life?"
"What is written in the Law?" he replied. "How do you read it?"
He answered: " 'Love the Lord your God with all your heart and with all your soul
and with all your strength and with all your mind'; and,
'Love your neighbor as yourself.'"
"You have answered correctly," Jesus replied. "Do this and you will live."
But he wanted to justify himself, so he asked Jesus, "And who is my neighbor?"

—Luke 10:25-29 (NIV)

This lawyer and I have much in common. I love to get the facts by testing what people are really thinking. I want the world to know that I'm right, so I justify myself frequently, restating what I said to be sure that I am understood. One of my great disappointments, growing up, was that I didn't attend a school with a debate team. I could talk fast, reason rapidly, cut opponents down to the quick—I'd have been good.

However, when people wanted to debate Jesus, he often refused, sometimes keeping silent or telling a parable. How does one debate with a story? A parable switched the conversation from me versus you to we're all in this together—how might we work at this situation? With whom do we identify? What are options for a real-life situation?

That's one of the problems with undocumented immigration—we're talking about 12 million real life situations, 12 million stories begging to be told. There is no 'one law fits all' answer to immigration reform. Overworked and under-resourced judges tasked with deciding who stays and who goes move as quickly as possible to shorten a horrendous backlog. They are often not consistent in their decisions, sending one parent away and allowing another in the exact situation to stay.

One Mennonite pastor recently told me that his congregation had compiled 300 pages of hardship documentation for an undocumented neighbor who was appealing her immigration status. The overly busy judge read only the top page before denying her citizenship and deporting her. This mother was the primary wage earner for her family, which includes a child with Down's Syndrome. The congregation now wonders how to support the family financially.

Some of the comments people make about immigration sound like justifications I tend to make when I'm worried about myself:

"My ancestors came legally." (I was here first.)

"They are taking our jobs away." (I don't want to share.)

"They won't learn English." (I don't trust people who aren't like me.)

But then I hear the stories—stories of farms lost because of NAFTA, of slavery (here or there), of not being able to return for funerals of one's beloved parents or see one's children for years.

There is a growing understanding among researchers that immigrants do not come to the United States merely because it is a "land of plenty" or to "fulfill the American dream." Most migrants would actually prefer to stay in their home countries where they have family, speak the language, and are already culturally integrated.

However, this is not always an option. Most undocumented immigrants come to the United States or overstay their visas for four overarching reasons: fleeing persecution, family reunification, economics, or some combination of the prior factors.

We also need to hear the stories of the people in Phoenix, the capital of kidnappings in the United States because of Mexican drug cartels operating there and coyotes wanting "back pay." Since it is nearly impossible to immigrate legally (waits from Mexico can be over 20 years), criminals offer a path that no one should have to take.

Across the United States, state after state is considering 'copycat' laws to the one in Arizona. Inhospitality is blowing from state to state. Our country of immigrants increasingly is saying "don't come" to the people who harvest our food, work in our restaurants and clean our hotels. Yes, we have an employment problem in our country, but my neighbor who used to install organs in churches is not planning to go to California to pick strawberries.

Two other people make an appearance in Jesus' parable—the priest and the Levite—the holy people who didn't want to soil their hands or break the law by becoming unclean or who had a busy schedule to keep. Friends, immigration is a problem for each of us in the United States. We can't walk by and think our family, our community, or our congregation isn't involved.

The Good Samaritan looks at the bruised and crumpled man lying on the road and doesn't question why he is there or why he made the stupid decision to travel a dangerous road. He cares for him, spends money on him. And Jesus says, "Go and do likewise."

—Susan Mark Landis

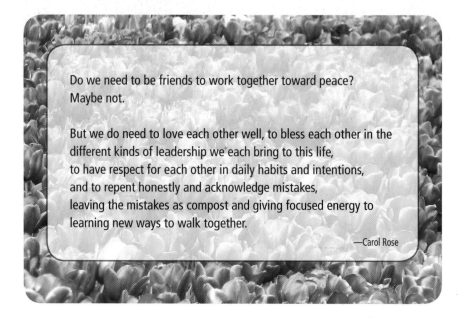

Do we need to be friends to work together toward peace?
Maybe not.

But we do need to love each other well, to bless each other in the different kinds of leadership we each bring to this life,
to have respect for each other in daily habits and intentions,
and to repent honestly and acknowledge mistakes,
leaving the mistakes as compost and giving focused energy to learning new ways to walk together.

—Carol Rose

Cynthia Friesen Coyle

God,
Calm the boiling within me
Cease my broiling of others
Call me to practice your grace and
Celebrate what's right with the world.
Amen.

—hjkh

Muffins and scones

"I have compassion for the crowd, because they have been with me now
for three days and have nothing to eat. If I send them away hungry to their homes,
they will faint on the way—and some of them have come from a great distance."

—Mark 8:1-8 (NRSV)

My son made an off-hand comment one day when thanking me for again sending chocolate chip cookies to him at college. "My friends identify you with something other than your peace job now," he said with relief.

We are all multi-faceted people. Sometimes the witness I make for Christian peacemaking is unpopular and I don't want that to be the sole definition of who I am. One way I try to offer another image is to freely share my baking, perhaps especially with people who disagree with me on issues deeply important to both of us.

When the young neighbor who grew up playing with my children had to serve an extra 60 days in Iraq, I was angry at the U.S. government. I protested against the war; he received mailings of chocolate chip cookies from me. He knew where I stood. I didn't enclose a note, just sent the sweets. I was invited to his homecoming party and he said mine were the best cookies he received while in Iraq. (The secret? I used the recipe on the back of Nestle semi-sweet chocolate chips, leaving out the nuts and adding a bit more flour. I slightly under-baked them in a disposable pan, cooled them, topped them with a second batch and a few slices of bread that fit under the pan lid, and immediately mailed them. I hoped the scorching Iraqi temperatures meant they would smell fresh out of the oven.)

My congregation and I have had some painful times. The last two years I've baked breads for our Winter Bible Institute Saturday morning meetings. Part of my reason I volunteered is that people who come out on a wintry morning deserve warm hospitality, but most of it is simply thanking my congregation, in a way I hope they understand, for claiming me through the hard times.

Calling this "feeding my enemies" isn't accurate. More, I'm trying to find a way to show people with whom I have deep-seated disagreements that I care about them. When I bake, I often pray for the people who will eat the goodies. It reminds me that they are more than their views with which I disagree. God had it right—pray for those who persecute you, and feed them while you're at it.

—*Susan Mark Landis*

Lemon-poppy seed scones

Servings: Makes 8 large scones or 16 sensibly sized ones

Ingredients
3 cups all purpose flour
1 cup white sugar
3 tablespoons poppy seeds
1 tablespoon baking powder
1 teaspoon salt
10 tablespoons (1 1/4 sticks) chilled unsalted butter, cut into small pieces
grated peel and juice of a large lemon (at least 2 teaspoons peel and 2 tablespoons juice, likely much more)
1 large egg
1/3 cup (or more) cream
Raw sugar, if you have

Preparation
Preheat oven to 375°F. Mix flour, 1 cup sugar, poppy seeds, baking powder, lemon peel, and salt in large bowl. Cut in butter, using two knives or a pastry blender, until mixture resembles coarse meal. Whisk egg and lemon juice in medium bowl to blend. Add to flour mixture. Mix with wooden spoon until moist clumps form. Add 1/3 cup cream (or a bit less). Stir just until dough comes together, adding more cream if dough seems dry. With floured hands, gather dough into ball. Flatten into 8-inch round (or two 6-inch rounds). Cut each round into 8 wedges. Transfer scones to large baking sheet; brush with cream.
Liberally sprinkle with raw sugar.
Bake until scones are golden brown and toothpick inserted into center comes out clean, about 25 minutes. Transfer to rack and cool.

—Susan Mark Landis

The great silence of the crows

Sing to the Lord with thanksgiving; make melody to our God on the lyre.
He covers the heavens with clouds, prepares rain for the earth,
makes grass grow on the hills.
He gives to the animals their food, and to the young ravens when they cry.

—Psalm 147:7-9 (NRSV)

We Benedictine monks have a special affinity for crows, which might seem rather odd, as many people find other birds to be more, well let's just say, lovable. But this affinity can be traced all the way back to our roots in the earliest period of Benedictine life. Only a generation after St. Benedict, St. Gregory the Great wrote what came to be known as "The Dialogues of St. Gregory the Great" with all of Book Two of The Dialogues being dedicated to the life of Benedict. In chapter eight, Gregory recounts a story of Benedict and a crow that has caught the imagination of Benedictines for 1,500 years.

In this story, we are told that Benedict had a habit of feeding a particular crow every day. But one day a nefarious character, "one Florentius, Priest of a church nearby...possessed with diabolical malice, began to envy the holy man's virtues, to back-bite his manner of living, and to withdraw as many as he could from going to visit him." His hatred for Benedict's virtue growing to such a degree, Florentius eventually sent a loaf of poisoned bread to Benedict. But our father Benedict, anchored in a life of prayer, perceived the evil intent and asked the crow whom he fed every day to take the loaf away and dispose of it, "where no man may find it." The crow did and has, since that day, held a special place in our hearts.

A legend? Perhaps. A truth? Definitely.

That truth is that all of creation participates in the Divine Plan, the plan that continually moves us forward in what is known as Salvation History. We are not alone: there are over six billion of God's children on earth who have all been created in God's image and likeness. There are untold numbers of animals, birds, fish, insects, trees, bushes, flowers, oceans, rivers, lakes, deserts, and so much more, that participate in God's plan of creation. This planet is filled with God's life in so many different and mysterious ways. And all of that life is a tiny glimpse of who and what God is.

Outside of the window of my cell, a number of crows gather each morning. The monastic day begins somewhat early in a continuation of the Greater Silence, which begins the night before at 9:00 pm and continues until 9:00 am. The purpose of The Greater Silence is the pursuit of peace and a holy life and for the avoidance of sin. It is, in fact, my favorite time of day. As the early dawn peaks over the horizon, it is, so often, the crows that "get up" first and seem to begin their loud morning praise.

In the past few weeks, with my window wide open, that morning praise of the crows has been impinging on my own silent meditation. At first, honestly, I was annoyed. In fact, the more annoyed I became, the louder they became. Or at least it seemed that way. Their "crowing" seemed almost painful and needlessly aggressive. This went on for days, then weeks, until one morning last week, I realized these crows had something to teach me about my own meditation. I realized that so often in my own silence, I am fighting, fighting the sounds of creation all around me and, much more distractingly, fighting all the sounds, thoughts, feelings, and noise in my own head. At times this could be downright violent; not physically violent, but emotionally violent. So much energy was being used to ward off any noise that I had no energy left to actually hear what nature, or my own thoughts, or especially God, had to say to me.

And so, I began to listen to the crows. And as I listened, I found myself becoming more peaceful. And as I became more peaceful, I found myself much more able to listen to God. And as I found myself much more able to listen to God, I found myself much more willing to share my little corner of the world with the crows.

And all of that seemed like a good lesson for a man who claims to have dedicated his life to peace. If we are to achieve peace before the sun goes down—that great Benedictine saying that I so love—then it seems to me we must begin by listening. When we listen, really listen to ourselves, our enemies, our friends, all of nature around us, we are listening to all of God's creation. When we listen, we learn that we can share our world. When we listen, we learn that we are in this together. When we listen, we learn that even the incessant "crowing" of our old friends, the crows, isn't so bad.

I wonder how many wars might have been avoided had we just listened to each other? I wonder how many oil spills could have been avoided had we just listened to nature? I'm going to keep on doing the work of wondering, because I believe our ability to wonder eventually leads us to listen. But from now on, I'm going to take some time to wonder—and listen—with the crows.

Pax.

—*Brother James Dowd*

Carol Penner

Peace cookies

Ingredients
1/2 cup butter—to soothe old wounds between nations
1 cup brown sugar—like the good earth we need to preserve
1 egg—from which life is given, not to be taken by war
1/2 cup milk—for the children, the same all over the world
1 teaspoon vanilla—for its pure and delicate nature
1 1/4 cup oats—harvested in August, the month Hiroshima is remembered with sorrow
1 1/4 cups flour—wheat sheaves tied, as nations united by strings of hope for peace
1/2 teaspoon each, salt and soda—to season your lives with kindness
1 teaspoon cinnamon—to spice up your life by working for peace
1/2 cup sesame seeds—for the many seeds of good will that can blossom into world peace
3/4 cup raisins, grapes dried in the sun—for a reminder that after a nuclear war, there could be a nuclear winter with no sun for years
3/4 cups M&Ms—for rainbow colors and promises to keep

Directions
Cream butter and sugar in large mixing bowl.
Add egg, milk, and vanilla. Mix well.
Add oats, flour, salt, soda, and cinnamon. Mix well.
Add sesame seeds, raisins, and M&Ms. Mix well.
Drop by spoonsful on ungreased baking sheet.
Bake at 350 ° F. for about 12 minutes. Makes about 3 dozen.

—Christine Dull, Dayton International Peace Center

June 29

Peace out!

*Let us therefore make every effort to do what leads to peace
and to mutual edification.*

—Romans 14:19 (NIV)

A special display of patriotic red, white, and blue tee-shirts for the
Fourth of July caught my eye as I looked around the KMart women's
department. One of the advertised designs was a red shirt with small
blue and white flowers in the shape of the circular 1960s peace symbol.

Wait a minute.

Has the symbol of the anti-war, anti-establishment, anti-government movement of the 1960s been co-opted as a "patriotic" symbol? I guess so. Since my
initial shock, I see that the peace symbol has become ubiquitous! At the local
Ten Thousand Villages store, new arrivals include peace symbol earrings made
from Ecuadorian tagua nuts and a peace symbol pin made from a recycled
Ghanaian Coca-Cola can. I have found sticky tab notes, buttons, refrigerator
magnets, sew-on patches, posters, and a decorated cake at the Elkhart County,
Indiana, 4-H Fair carrying the peace symbol. At the local gas station, among
the refrigerated drinks are cans of peace tea, with not only the peace symbol
but several speech bubbles containing anti-establishment comments. So are we
having a worldwide patriotic movement toward peace or something?

Later, I purposely went to another KMart to look further and found more
tee shirts as well as jackets covered with peace signs, but hearts and butterflies were also popular. Hmmm, I thought. Let's check out the men and boys'
department. Here was another Fourth of July display of tee-shirts. Were there
also red, white, and blue peace symbols, hearts, and butterflies there? Not on
your life! Here were more manly things, such as an antlered deer and camouflage designs. Okay. I get the picture. Patriotic peace is a girly-girly thing, but
definitely not a he-man thing.

It is interesting that British artist Gerald Holtom created the peace symbol
in 1958 to represent nuclear disarmament for an anti-nuclear war march in

London, and it spread from there. He used the semaphore flag signals for the letters N and D, two flags held in an upside down V-shape and two flags held with one straight up, and the other straight down, respectively. These two signal shapes were combined inside a circle.

Visual symbols can be powerful, and here's an opportunity to participate in using one recognized worldwide. As Christian peacemakers, how might we witness to its original meaning as a serious anti-war symbol, and declare its true relevance for today? "Let us conduct ourselves in ways that lead to peace and mutual growth," the Apostle Paul says in Romans 14:19. Can you find ways to use this symbol to again lead to thoughts of peace and mutual growth while celebrating Martin Luther King, Jr. Day, Valentine's Day, or Easter? Be part of a *real* worldwide movement toward peace. Brainstorm and use your creativity to peace out!

—Beth Berry

Judith Baer Kulp

June 30

Pro-life

"For your own lifeblood I will surely require a reckoning:
from every animal I will require it and from human beings,
each one for the blood of another, I will require a reckoning for human life."

—Genesis 9:5 (NRSV)

As God spoke to Noah, making a new covenant "with [him] and [his] descendants…and with every living creature" there was the expectation that neither humans nor animals were free to take life except for food.

Later, in the Decalogue, God would reaffirm His prohibition against taking life by telling Moses, "You shall not [kill]" (Exodus 20:13). Jesus expanded on this commandment in Matthew 5:21-24, explaining that we ought to refrain from anger, insults, and name calling as these often lead to violence and even killing. Instead, we should actively seek reconciliation with those we have offended or who have offended us.

It is not uncommon for Christians to equate a "pro-life" belief with the issue of abortion only.

"You shall not kill" is logically applied to this issue for those who believe that human life begins at conception. But there are many other situations in which God may "require a reckoning…for the blood of another." Some of these include capital punishment, war, unjust economic practices, and accumulation of wealth in the face of poverty.

These and other situations can and do result in the loss of life. To the degree that we participate in these practices, or allow them to continue, we are responsible for the loss of human life.

While most of us can assert that we are not actively killing, nevertheless through ignorance, unconcern, fear, or selfishness we may contribute to the loss of human life.

As we embrace a more holistic "pro-life" ethic, we must be aware of what is going on in the world: following local and national news, and to some degree being aware of practices and situations that cause suffering and death. Then if ssible we ought to take action to relieve suffering and possibly prevent death, or advocate for changes in policies and practices that cause death, either directly or indirectly.

As we allow, God's Holy Spirit will heighten our awareness and lead us to specific actions. As followers of Christ and worshipers of God, let us commit to embracing a theology of life that extends the sanctity of life to all issues and situations in which life is threatened and to letting this broad theology of life direct our actions and choices.

—Tom Beutel

A new look at life

Recently there were a couple of very scary spiders who took up residence outside my front door. My first instinct was to kill them. I quickly realized that I desired their death, not because I found them so threatening and offensive, but because I was afraid of them, and that I feared them because of the way they looked. I decided to let them live, and found that I wanted them to live, because they reminded me of the necessity of coexisting peacefully with others, despite our differences.

—Audrey Hindes DiPalma

Appendices

Seasoned with Peace

Judith Baer Kulp

On your path to peace, pause on our web site for:

printouts of craft projects
links to additional resources
conversations with contributors
information about how to submit entries to Seasoned With Peace
a blog
how to order books

www.seasonedwithpeace.com

Bible reference index

Old Testament

New Testament

continued on p. 270

Appendix 2
Recipes and crafts index

Appendix 3
Contributor index

Appendix 4
Quotations and sources index

p. viii—Henry David Thoreau, Journal, 1853.

p. 1—Joan Chittister, O.S.B., *The Rule of Benedict: Insights for the Ages*, (Crossroad Publishing Company: 1992).

p. 5—Henri Nouwen and John M. Dear (ed.), *The Road to Peace*, (Orbis Books: 2002).

p. 37, 45—For more information about Agent Orange, see http://www.vnagentorange.org.

p. 37—Gene Knudsen Hoffman, *Fellowship: the Journal of The Fellowship of Reconciliation*, May/June 1997.

p. 67—P.J. O'Rourke, *All the Trouble in the World: The Lighter Side of Overpopulation, Famine, Ecological Disaster, Ethnic Hatred, Plague, and Poverty*, (Atlantic Monthly Press: 1995).

p. 103—Jon Twitchell, Pastor Jon's Lectionary Journal, http://www.yourchurchweb.net/PastorJon/2006/04/holy-week-quote-to-consider_10.html.

p. 109—Rainer Maria Rilke, *Sonnets to Orpheus XXI (First Part)*.

p. 130—Mother's Day Proclamation by Julia Ward Howe, 1870.

p. 146—Thomas Merton, *New Seeds of Contemplation,* (New Directions Publishing Corporation: 1992).

p. 151—Edwin Markham, "Outwitted," from *The Shoes of Happiness, and Other Poems* (1913).

p. 152—"100,000 Excess Iraqi Deaths Since War – Study", Reuters, October 28, 2004, http://www.commondreams.org/headlines04/1028-08.htm.

p. 176-178—Gabriel Schlabach worked for the Mennonite Central Committee Washington Office from 2007-2009, where he advocated to the U.S. government on a variety of issues, including civil rights and religious freedom.

p. 184-185—for a more in-depth discussion of God's nature in relation to evil from a similar perspective, read the final chapter of Thomas Jay Oord's *Defining Love: A Philosophical, Scientific, and Theological Engagement* from Brazos Press.

p. 186-187—Henri J.M. Nouwen, "The Companionship of the Dead," August 29, *Bread for the journey: a daybook of wisdom and faith,* (HarperOne: 2006).

p. 192—Source: US EPA: http://media.mgbg.com/wkrg/photos/weather/downloads/Water_Facts.pdf

p. 197—Sources include Ervin Stutzman, Glen Alexander Guyton, Joanna Shenk, Sylvia Morrison, and Anne Bishop. A longer version and links at internet blog - "Oppression is bad, now what?" by Tim Nafziger and Mark Van Steenwyk, The Mennonite, 9/26/2010. http://www.themennonite.org/bloggers/timjn/posts/Oppression_is_bad_now_what.

p. 207—J. Philip Newell, *Celtic Prayer from Iona*, (Paulist Press: 1997).

Appendix 5

Compilers

Lisa J. Amstutz is a freelance writer, coauthor of *Local Choices*, author of two forthcoming picture books, and editor of *PeaceSigns* e-zine. She homeschools four children with big brown eyes, shares six acres with a hodgepodge of small livestock, and often grabs a camera to walk and relax. Lisa is always up for a cup of tea, a good book, or a game of euchre. She is married to Michael Amstutz and is a member of Sonnenberg Mennonite Church in Kidron, Ohio.

Susan Mark Landis is passionate in living life, baking bread, and drinking tea. She tends her perennial flower beds and knits as she prays over the issues of the day. Susan has served in Mennonite peace and justice staff positions since 1995 and is author of *But Why Don't We Go to War? Finding Jesus' Path to Peace.* She is wife to the ever-patient and resourceful Dennis Landis, mother of Laura and Joel who still appreciate her chocolate chip cookies and editing skills, and a member of Oak Grove Mennonite Church in Smithville, Ohio.

Cindy Snider is a freelance writer, author of the children's novel *Finding Anna Bee*, and coauthor of *Don't Be Afraid, Stories of Christians in Times of Trouble*. She is a Georgia peach in all the best ways, travels whenever possible, has pirate heroes, is an encourager to one and all, and a member of Mennonite Church of the Servant in Wichita, Kansas.

Judith Baer Kulp thought she had retired from publishing after years in pre-computer daily and weekly newsrooms and two decades of print and web publishing in the international/global learning offices at the University of North Texas in Denton. However, she couldn't resist *Seasoned with Peace*. She lives with her husband, Lowell, at Lake Kiowa, Texas. She putters among heat-resistant perennials and tries to grow tomatoes like those in northwest Ohio where they grew up. Judith carries shoulder bags big enough for cameras and books, often on road trips to visit four daughters and seven grandchildren in Texas, Arizona, Wyoming, and Ohio.

A blessing at the closing of spring

Jeanne Zimmerly Jantzi

"Don't cry because it's over.
Smile because it happened."

—Dr. Seuss